Great Barrier Reef
0 200 km
0 200 miles
SOUTH PACIFIC OCEAN
CORAL SEA
Great Barrier Reef
Cooktown
13
Dunbar
Port Douglas
Cairns
Innisfail
Croydon
Einasleigh
Hinchinbrook Island
Ingham
Great Dividing Range
Townsville
Bowen
Whitsunday I.
9
Julia Creek
Charters Towers
Hughenden
Mackay
Moranbah
Townshend I.
Winton
Clermont
Rockhampton
Longreach
Barcaldine
Emerald
Gladstone
Blackall
Biloela
Bundagerg
8
Fraser Island
Windorah
Queensland
Charleville
Roma
Gympie
Brisbane
Noccundra
Toowoomba
Eulo
Southport
Tenterfield
New South Wales
Ballina

Central Brisbane
0 500 m
0 500 yds
ROMA STREET PARKLAND
Countess Street
Fareland Blvd
PETRIE TERRACE
Roma Street Railway Station
Roma Street
Albert Street
Wickham Terrace
Birley Street
Astor Terrace
Wharf Street
Turbot Street
St John's Anglican Cathedral
Central Station
Old Windmill
Roma Street Forum
Ann Street
Adelaide St
Masonic Memorial Temple
Customs House
1
Riverside Centre
Anzac Memorial
Creek Street
Eagle Street
Queen Street
Riparian Plaza
Herschel St
George Street
Tank St
Museum of Brisbane
Brisbane Arcade
Edward Street
St Stephen's Cathedral
Eagle Street Pier
William Jolly Bridge
North Quay
Turbot Street
City Hall
Regal Theatre
Riverside Expressway
Burnett Lane
CITY
Waterfront Place
Kurilpa Bridge
Gallery of Modern Art (GoMA)
Myer Centre
Elizabeth Street
Albert Street
Charlotte Street
Queensland State Library
Boardwalk
Treasury Building
Festival Hall
Mary Street
former Naval Offices
Hope Street
Queensland Art Gallery
Victoria Bridge
former State Library Building
George Street
William Street
Margaret Street
Peel St
Grey Street
Queensland Museum
Royal Historical Society
Commissariat Store
Alice Street
Fish Lane
Melbourne St
Queensland Performing Arts Centre (QPAC)
Wheel of Brisbane
Brisbane River
CITY BOTANIC GARDENS
South Brisbane Railway Station
Parliament House
SOUTH BRISBANE
Riverside Promenade
SOUTH BANK PARKLAND
Gardens Point Road
Queensland University of Technology
Brisbane Convention & Exhibition Centre
Suncorp Piazza
Russell St
Cordelia Street
Merivale Street
Glenelg St
Little Stanley Street
William Robinson Gallery
QUT Garden Theatre
MUSGRAVE PARK
South Bank Cinemas and IMAX Complex
Streets Beach
Jagera Arts Centre
Ernest St
Colchester Street
Tribune Street
South Brisbane Railway Station
D0315689

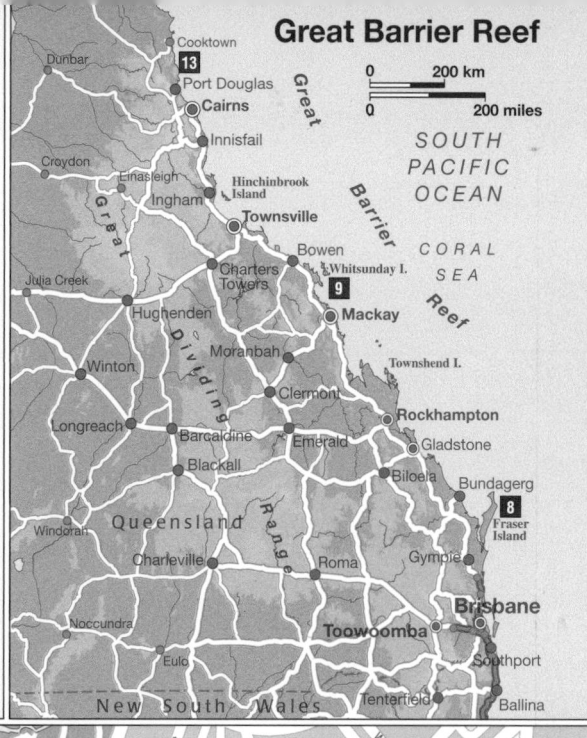

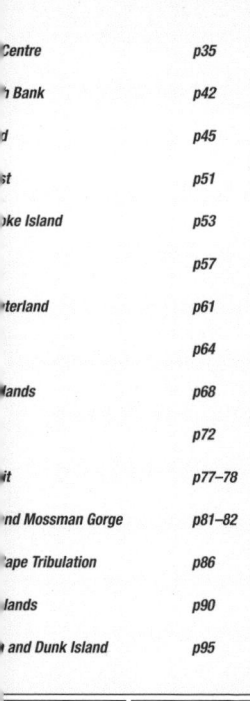

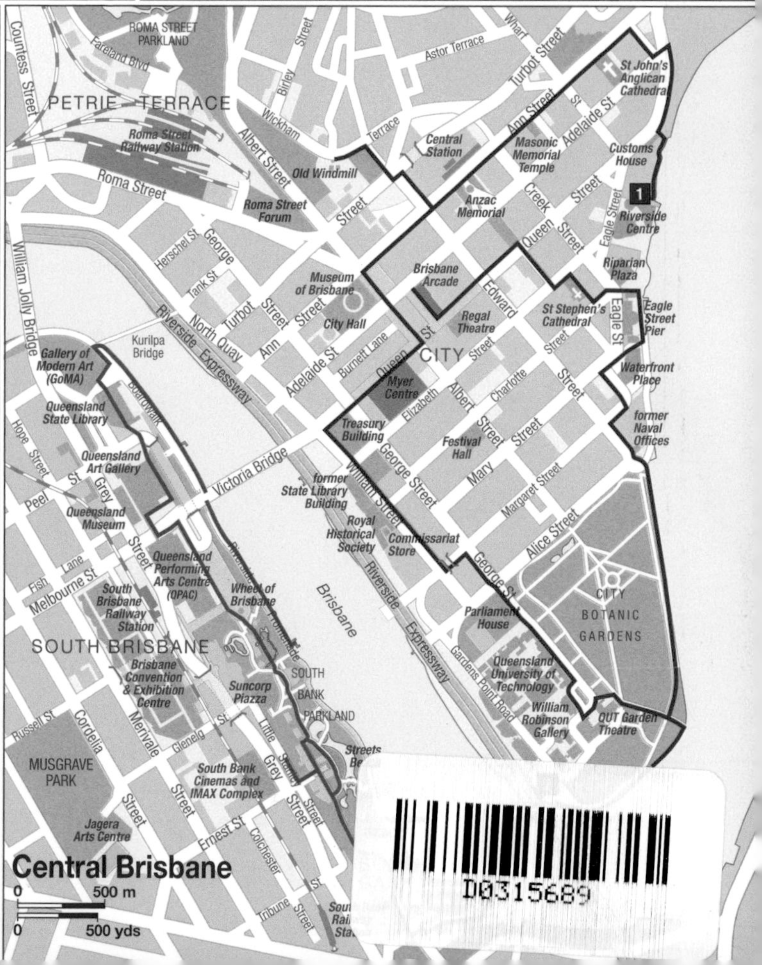

INSIGHT GUIDES

BRISBANE, CAIRNS
AND THE GREAT BARRIER REEF
Step by Step

APA PUBLICATIONS
Part of the Langenscheidt Publishing Group

CONTENTS

Introduction

Overview

Walks and Tours

Directory

Credits and Index

ABOUT THIS BOOK

This *Step by Step Guide* has been produced by the editors of Insight Guides, whose books have set the standard for visual travel guides since 1970. With top-quality photography and authoritative recommendations, this guidebook brings you the very best of Brisbane, Cairns and the Great Barrier Reef in a series of 15 tailor-made tours.

WALKS AND TOURS

The tours in the book provide something to suit all budgets, tastes and trip lengths. Focusing on the hubs of Brisbane and Cairns, their hinterlands and selected coastal attractions in between, they embrace a range of interests, so whether you are a shopaholic, a gourmet, a lover of the big outdoors or have kids to entertain, you will find an option to suit.

We recommend reading the whole of a tour before setting out. This should help you to familiarise yourself with the route and plan where to stop for refreshments – options for this are shown in the 'Food and Drink' boxes, recognisable by the knife-and-fork sign, on most pages.

For our pick of the walks by theme, consult Recommended Tours For... *(see pp.6–7)*.

OVERVIEW

The tours are set in context by this introductory section, giving an overview of the region to set the scene, plus background information on food and drink, shopping, entertainment, Gold Coast theme parks and the Great Barrier Reef. A succinct history timeline highlights the key events that have shaped this part of Queensland over the centuries.

DIRECTORY

Also supporting the tours is a Directory chapter, comprising a user-friendly, clearly organised A–Z of practical information, our pick of where to stay while you are in and around Brisbane, Cairns and the Great Barrier Reef, and select restaurant listings; these eateries complement the more low-key cafés and restaurants that feature within the tours and are intended to offer a wider choice for evening dining. Also included here are some nightlife listings.

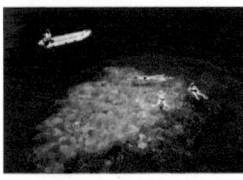

Above: the Glass House Mountains are inland from the Sunshine Coast; Queensland Club in Brisbane; Skyrail Rainforest Cableway to Kuranda; snorkelling at the Great Barrier Reef; Brisbane's Streets Beach.

The Author

Lindsay Brown is a former marine biologist who now divides his time between Australia and South Asia writing travel guides and taking photos for various international publishers. Lindsay has dived on the reef, camped in the Whitsundays, ridden the Pacific's swells and driven Queensland's outback roads. What he loves most about Queensland are the empty spaces, vibrant light and uncompromisingly relaxed attitude of Queenslanders. Additional input was provided by Cathy Finch, a Queensland-based writer and photographer, and some of the tours were originally conceived by long-time resident Paul Phelan.

Margin Tips
Shopping tips, historical facts, handy hints and information on activities help visitors to make the most of their time in Brisbane, Cairns and the Great Barrier Reef.

Feature Boxes
Notable topics are highlighted in these special boxes.

Key Facts Box
This box gives details of the distance covered on the tour, plus an estimate of how long it should take. It also states where the route starts and finishes, and gives key travel information such as which days are best to do the route or handy transport tips.

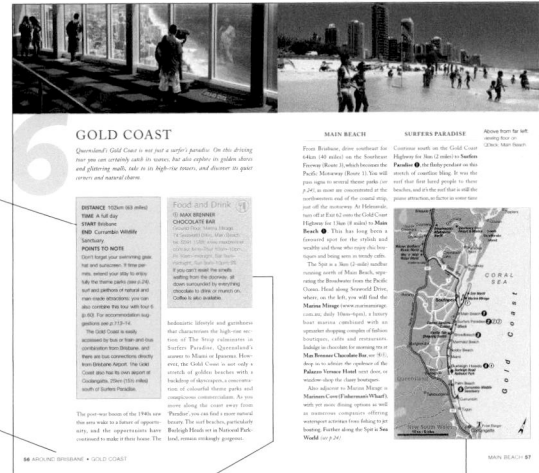

Footers
Look here for the tour name, a map reference and the main attraction on the double-page.

Food and Drink
Recommendations of where to stop for refreshment are given in these boxes. The numbers prior to each restaurant/café name link to references in the main text. Restaurants in the Food and Drink boxes are plotted on the maps.

The $ signs at the end of each entry reflect the approximate cost of a two-course meal for one, with a glass of house wine. These should be seen as a guide only. Price ranges, also quoted on the inside back flap for easy reference, are:

$$$	over A$60
$$	A$40–60
$	below A$40

Route Map
Detailed cartography shows the tour clearly plotted with numbered dots. For more detailed mapping, see the pull-out map slotted inside the back cover.

ADVENTURE-SEEKERS

With careful preparation, steer your own 4WD adventure on the world's largest sand islands of Moreton (tour 3), North Stradbroke (tour 5) and Fraser (tour 8), or take to the waves when surf's up on the Sunshine Coast (tour 4) or the Gold Coast

RECOMMENDED TOURS FOR...

ANIMAL-LOVERS

Hand-feed a wild dolphin at Tangalooma (tour 3), dive or snorkel the world's greatest living reef (tours 9 and 10, *and p.26*), and get up close to a crocodile in safety at Australia Zoo (tour 4).

CHILDREN

Whether you are based in Brisbane, with its urban beach and Big Wheel (walk 2), or the beach mecca of the Gold Coast (tour 6), it is easy to access the fun-packed theme parks *(see p.24)*.

CULTURE

For music, international exhibitions, or indigenous and modern art, Brisbane (walks 1 and 2) and Cairns (walk 10) have galleries and art centres that showcase Queensland culture.

FOOD AND DRINK

Brisbane's standout bistros (walk 1) grill seriously succulent steaks. For seafood you can't beat Noosa's Hasting Street eateries (tour 4), and Australia's best coffee is grown and brewed on the Atherton Tablelands (tour 14).

HISTORIANS

See Queensland's oldest windmill plus the former penal colony's commissariat store in Brisbane (walk 1), and ride the engineering marvel of the Kuranda Scenic Railway (tour 11), completed in 1891.

NATIONAL PARKS

Strap on the walking shoes and hit the trails of Queensland's lush national parks on the Sunshine Coast (tour 4), Gold Coast Hinterland (tour 7), Atherton Tablelands (tour 14) and en route to Mission Beach (tour 15).

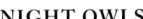

NIGHT OWLS

In Brisbane enjoy a night out at the theatre in the renowned Queensland Performing Arts Complex at South Bank (walk 2) or find a riverside bar (walk 1). In Cairns (walk 10) visit the casino and the Tanks Art Centre.

ROBINSON CRUSOES

Find peace and solitude on an almost deserted tropical island among the Whitsunday Islands (tour 9). Similar seclusion can be found on the endless empty beaches of North Stradbroke Island (tour 5).

SCUBA-DIVERS

Experienced divers and first-timers will be amazed by the coral gardens and kaleidoscopic marine life of the Great Barrier Reef *(see p.26)* near Cairns (walk 10) and the Whitsunday Islands (tour 9).

OVERVIEW

An overview of Queensland's geography, character and culture, plus illuminating background information on food and drink, shopping, entertainment, theme parks, the Great Barrier Reef and history.

INTRODUCTION

From the glittering Gold Coast and bustling capital city of Brisbane to the verdant Wet Tropics, where prehistoric rainforest meets the greatest coral reef on earth, Queensland's amazing coastline is an unrivalled adventure playground and idyllic escape.

Size isn't everything, but it is a factor when considering Queensland. This may be only the second-largest state in Australia (after Western Australia), but its 1.73 million sq km (667,000 sq miles) would comfortably swallow several European countries. However, within this vast area there are only 4.4 million people; about equivalent to the population of Sydney. For the visitor it can still seem busy and hectic since so many are drawn to the high-rise high-gratification zone of the Gold Coast and cosmopolitan Brisbane, where crowds are part of the atmosphere. Anywhere else, though, and this is one relaxed, uncrowded and friendly place.

GEOGRAPHY AND LAYOUT

The region covered in this book is the coast, hinterland and offshore islands between Brisbane and the Gold Coast in the south and Daintree and Cape Tribulation in the north. The tours begin with two walks exploring the historic, entertainment and scenic precincts of the Queensland capital. On Brisbane's doorstep, the natural sand

islands of Moreton and North Stradbroke offer scenic 4WD exploration and marine wildlife encounters. Also an easy day trip from Brisbane are the high-rise-backed beaches of the Gold Coast and their counterpoint, the verdant Gold Coast hinterland. The Gold Coast is also the setting for a cluster of theme parks *(see pp.24–5)*.

Heading north, the Sunshine Coast combines an idyllic climate and landscape with gourmet culture, while Fraser Island has a highway of sand for 4WD enthusiasts. In the picturesque Whitsunday Islands leave your car behind as you island-hop by ferry, camp under the stars and spend your days kayaking and snorkelling.

In Cairns, the capital of far north Queensland with unsurpassed access to the Great Barrier Reef, explore the historic town on foot. From Cairns, you can take a ride on a historic train and amazing cable car to and from the market town of Kuranda or explore the resorts of Port Douglas and Mission Beach, the ancient rainforests of Daintree and Cape Tribulation, and the coffee plantations and waterfalls of the Atherton Tablelands.

Coastal Fringe Dwellers
Almost two-thirds of Queensland's 3.5 million population live within 100km (60 miles) of Brisbane; the coastal strip north to Port Douglas accounts for the majority of the remainder.

HISTORY AND POLITICS

About 15 million years ago, the Australian continent broke away from an ancient land mass known as Gondwanaland and gradually drifted northwards to its present location. Due to periodic ice ages, sea levels were lower than today; so low that anyone reaching New Guinea from Asia could continue the journey to north Queensland on foot. These first migrants, ancestors of Australia's Aborigines, arrived some 50,000 years ago.

The First Europeans

Some historians argue that Portuguese mariners charted the northern coastline of Queensland as early as the 16th century, but it is Dutchman Willem Janssen, who sailed into the Gulf of Carpentaria in 1605, who is generally cited as the first European to 'discover' Australia. Another Dutchman, Abel Tasman, charted parts of Tasmania in 1642 and the northern coast from Cape York to Port Hedland two years later. However, credit for charting the eastern coastline goes to Captain James Cook, whose 1770 voyage opened the way to colonisation.

The Penal Years

The east coast of Australia became a dumping-ground for Britain's criminals. In 1788 and 1790 fleets of convict ships arrived at Port Jackson, Sydney's great harbour-to-be, and the colony grew. In 1799 Lieutenant Matthew Flinders charted much of Moreton Bay but failed to notice the mouth of the Brisbane River. The honour of 'discovering' the Brisbane River fell to three convicts and, soon after, a new penal settlement was established in Moreton Bay.

An Independent Queensland

The first half of the 19th century saw a change in European settlement in Australia. The transportation of convicts was phased out, and by 1860 the continent had been divided into seven colonies, one of which was Queensland. At that time the European population numbered only 23,520, and no industry had yet been established, although gold had been discovered in 1858.

Above from far left: Brisbane's CBD skyline and Story Bridge; hang-gliding off the coast near Port Douglas.

Below: high-rise Gold Coast viewed from QDeck.

Below: the endangered, flightless cassowary can be sighted in Queensland; koala at a sanctuary in Brisbane.

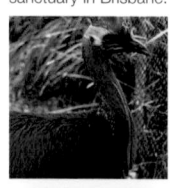

Federation, War and Depression

The Commonwealth of Australia, which included the state of Queensland, was born in 1901 and Brisbane was proclaimed a city the following year. When Britain declared war on Germany in August 1914, Australia, as a member of the British Empire, was automatically at war, too. In 1923 vast silver-lead-zinc deposits were found inland at Mount Isa, but the Depression of the late 1920s and early 1930s was hard on Queensland. In 1934 the Labor Party stimulated the economy through large capital projects, including the construction of Story Bridge and the University of Queensland.

War and Boom Times

When Britain went to war against Germany in September 1939, Australia once more automatically entered the conflict. Of the 1 million Australian servicemen and women who had enlisted, almost 27,000 died.

The 1950s saw the rapid development of the coastal strip south of Brisbane. Originally a secluded holiday destination for the Brisbane middle classes, its property values soared in the post-war period, leading one journalist to dub the area the 'Gold Coast'.

Modern Politics

The long tradition of Labor politics in Queensland fell apart in the mid-1950s. After 25 years in power, the party lost the election, ushering in 32 years of rule by the National Party. For two decades until 1987, politics and social life in Queensland were dominated by Sir Joh Bjelke-Petersen, whose era was characterised by confrontation with unions and civil-rights advocates.

When Labor's Peter Beattie, victorious in the 2001 and 2004 elections, retired in 2007 he handed the premiership to Anna Bligh, Queensland's first female premier, who become the first woman to lead her party to a state election victory in 2009.

CLIMATE

Queensland has just two seasons: summer (Oct–Mar) and winter. The difference is more pronounced in the south. In the north, there is a wet season (mid-Dec–Apr), when rainfall and thunderstorms are common and there are occasional tropical cyclones. April to September during the Australian autumn and winter is often the best time to visit Queensland (particularly the north), as rainfall and temperatures are lower.

Brisbane has summer temperatures that range from 20°C to the high 30s (68–86°F plus) and winter temperatures of 10–20°C (35–68°F), with a daily average of eight hours of sunshine. In Cairns the temperature range in winter is 16–26°C (55–90°F) and in summer it can exceed 36°C (125°F), when humidity is also high.

POPULATION AND ECONOMY

According to the 2006 census, about 128,000 Aborigines and Torres Strait Islanders live in Queensland, which is 3.3 percent of the total population (*see feature*). Queensland has one of the fastest-growing populations of any state in Australia. Part of this increase is from overseas migration; Queensland's primary industries – wheat, fruit, cattle, cotton, sugar cane, viticulture, wool and mining – have largely depended on the hard work of immigrants from more than 200 nations. Some have congregated, creating atmospheric and vibrant neighbourhoods, such as South Sea Islanders in Mackay and Italians in Innisfail. However, it is the interstate migrants who are changing Queensland most dramatically. They include a lot of prosperous southern baby-boomers and retirees bringing their wealth north to buy property along the coast.

The influx has coloured the way the rest of Australia views Queenslanders. Historically, the typical Queenslander was defined by the rugged frontier of the far north and outback, with iconic pioneering status as well as conservative values. Another type resides in the southeast corner, a haven for retirees, where poker machines munch through pensions and high-rises shoot up to go one better than their neighbour.

FUTURE CHALLENGES

There are thousands of kilometres of Queensland coast where anyone can find their own little piece of paradise. Coastal Queensland has boomed on the back of tourism that understandably relies heavily on the state's natural wonders, particularly the Great Barrier Reef, but there are real threats to the idyllic image. Global warming has been implicated in recent coral-bleaching events, mining and agriculture add to harmful sediment flows, and the 2010 grounding of a wayward Chinese coal-carrying vessel has highlighted the growing challenges of conserving the beauty in a rapidly developing Queensland.

Indigenous Queensland

There is no escaping the fact that the Aboriginal people of Queensland have had a tragic existence since white settlement: killed in huge numbers by imported diseases and settlers' guns, living at the mercy of discriminatory laws and damaged by displacement, alcohol and drugs. There have been decades of government funding and more recently there has been official recognition of the mistakes of the past, but many policies have been misguided or mismanaged, and Aboriginal people still have a life expectancy many years less than that of the white community.

Among the many Queensland indigenous notables are the late poet and activist Kath Walker (whose traditional name is Oodgeroo Noonuccal), William Barton, the Brisbane-based Aboriginal didgeridoo player, the artist Judy Watson, and high-profile achievers such as Olympic gold medallist Cathy Freeman and television personality Ernie Dingo.

FOOD AND DRINK

Queensland's gastronomic credentials are born of two factors: a cultural diversity attracting chefs experienced in some of the world's most mouth-watering cuisines, plus the rich variety of the produce from Queensland's tropical seas, rolling pastures and volcanic soils.

It would be easy to draw the unkind conclusion that Australia does not possess a culinary style of its own; but it should be remembered that the country has evolved through little more than 200 years of immigration from almost every country in the world, and that the resulting blend of cultures has enriched its dining tables with a huge diversity of cross-cultural concepts. Although British immigrants were in the majority in the early days, Australia's menus were much enhanced by major waves of immigration from China, Italy, Greece and, more recently, Southeast Asia, the Middle East and Africa. In deference to the generally warm subtropical climate, there is now a definite avoidance of some of the heavy, stodgy menus of northern Europe.

The resultant fusion of disparate influences, which tends to disrespect culinary borders, is usually termed modern Australian or 'Mod Oz'. Thus, for example, Asian greens may accompany a Spanish-style seafood dish, the chef relying on the compatibility of the flavours and fresh local ingredients rather than traditional cuisine.

LOCAL CUISINE

The original local cuisine would be have to be 'bush tucker': seasonally available native plants and animals cooked over a campfire. The easiest way to sample these flavours in an authentic way is to join an Aboriginal-guided tour or attend an indigenous entertainment venue where bush tucker is on the menu. Alternatively, many of Queensland's more experimental chefs are infusing their dishes with native herbs and spices, while kangaroo, emu and crocodile are now commonly found on a Queensland menu.

There was a time when beef or lamb and 'three veg' would have summed up a typical Queensland dinner. But those times are long gone. There was also a time when a steak was a steak and the bigger the better. Not any more. You are as likely to find that your steak comes from a steer raised on the cool green pastures of Tasmania as from a dusty feed lot out of Rockhampton. Your waiter will hopefully be patient while you decide between 400-day-old, grass-fed Angus from

Coffee Break
Queensland's café scene has undergone a huge boom over the last few years. Expert local coffee roasters including Merlo and Di Bella have helped fuel the boom, as has a move towards alfresco eating. Coffee Club is a popular chain of cafés (many with free WiFi), attracting a varied and loyal clientele.

King Island or 300-day-old Wagyu with 160 days of grain feeding to promote the marbling of the fat. 'Healthy fat', you will be told. Then there is the decision of which cut of steak to choose and whether to cook it blue, rare or medium. A quality steak restaurant will never offer to cook a steak 'well done'. Just don't ask!

When it comes to seafood, few places on earth can claim to be superior to Queensland. Whatever your taste – be it molluscan, crustacean or piscatorial – Queensland has ample varieties and copious quantities sourced from clean waters. When in Brisbane, ask for Moreton Bay bugs: delicious slipper lobsters with excellent sweet white flesh, perfect for Mediterranean and Asian cooking styles. Up north, two species of fish, barramundi and coral trout, vie for top spot in a long list of delicious contenders. Barramundi or 'barra' is an estuarine perch that grows to legendary size and is excellent eating 'bush tucker'-style cooked in hot coals, or on a BBQ plate, or even as fish and chips. Coral trout is a beautiful, spotted tropical reef fish that perfectly suits Asian cuisine.

WHERE TO EAT

Brisbane claims the highest number of restaurants per capita of any city in Australia and has several neighbourhoods and streets that have evolved a popular restaurant scene, offering variety and informality along with quality and reasonable prices. The cafés and bistros of Park Road, Milton; Brunswick Street, Fortitude Valley; Merthyr Road, New Farm; and Little Stanley Street, South Bank, offer reasonable fare in often sophisticated settings. Most Brisbane precincts have a growing selection of ethnic restaurants, the most common being Thai, Indian and Vietnamese. Asian restaurants are mainly concentrated in Fortitude Valley, West End and Sunnybank.

The Gold Coast has more than 5,000 restaurants, ranging from super-casual surf club bistros, such as Northcliffe Surf Club Bistro, to opulent high-rise dining rooms. Noosa has a reputation for quality dining in modish restaurants usually found on or near sophisticated Hastings Street, Noosa Heads.

Above from far left: Aboriginal 'bush bread'; barramundi.

Below: smoked spanner crab ravioli at the Ochre Restaurant in Cairns.

Bring Your Own

If you are spooked by licensed-restaurant wine prices, it is usually not too hard to find an unlicensed BYO (bring your own wine) restaurant. BYO restaurants normally charge corkage (per person or per bottle) and don't allow BYO beer, but it is still much cheaper than buying massively marked-up wine – and there is often a strategically placed liquor outlet nearby.

Below: Gold Coast cocktail.

High-end Restaurants

Fine dining is almost exclusively found in the larger commercial centres and upmarket resorts – the sorts of places where you will also find five-star hotels, such as Brisbane, the Gold Coast, Noosa and Cairns along with the resort islands. And you do not have to look far past the dining rooms of the five-stars to find award-winning chefs performing culinary art for the grateful, and well-heeled, clientele. Brisbane's Cha Cha Char Wine Bar & Grill continues to raise the bar with quality, award-winning steaks, and the Gold Coast's Absynthe delights gourmands with Gallic ingenuity.

Ethnic Restaurants

The explosion in inexpensive ethnic cuisine in Australia shows no sign of stopping. Even global financial crises cannot stem the trend to eat out on a budget. Indian, Thai, Turkish, Mexican, Lebanese and Vietnamese have joined the old guard of Italian, Greek and Chinese to rescue folks from resorting to fast food or DIY home cooking. Away from the coast the choice may be limited to Chinese and pizza, but coastal Queensland, with its cosmopolitan population and massive tourist market, offers a staggering array of ethnic cuisine. Many restaurateurs maximise the cultural experience with careful attention to detail, such as the Ottoman-tent ambience at Ahmets in Brisbane's South Bank.

Pubs and Bistros

Again, it is the demands of inbound and international tourism that has boosted coastal Queensland's pubs from mere fuel stops to purveyors of quality food. Along the backpacker trail are barn-sized pubs selling steaks to BBQ yourself or placed on a hot volcanic rock. Both are fun, if rather odd, trends, whereby the expertise in timing is left to you, the novice, rather than a professional cook. Elsewhere, you will find many a gracious old pub that has been gentrified into a restaurant with an attached bar, rather than the other way round, such as the Straddie pub and Port Douglas's Court House Hotel.

DRINKS

Non-Alcoholic Drinks

Great coffee is grown on the Atherton Tablelands near Cairns, and there are plenty of cafés around that support the local growers and roasters. Throughout Queensland, fresh juice bars have become very common, and these are ideal places to find your favourite tropical juices to beat the heat.

Wine

The reputation of Australian wines has now fully matured. Australia has in excess of 2,500 wineries, many offering 'cellar-door' sales. While the biggest 20 companies produce over 95 percent of Australia's total output, 'boutique wineries' make up well over two-thirds of the total number of wineries. Some are found in Queensland, whose emerging wine industry (www.queenslandwine.com.au) includes fruit wines from the far north and award-winning reds and whites from southeast Queensland, especially in the area called the Granite Belt. Queensland wines are often light, crisp and fruity, and designed to complement Queensland's food.

Many consider the best oak-driven reds or whites to come from the oldest-established wine-growing area of Barossa Valley in South Australia, while the Hunter Valley is highly popular for its fruity Chardonnay and aged Semillons. The finest red varietals are Cabernet Sauvignon from Coonawarra in the southeast of South Australia, Shiraz from Heathcote in Victoria and Pinot Noir from Tasmania.

Beer

Australian beers are famous internationally, and are consumed in vast quantities by their domestic devotees. The most popular brew in Queensland is the local XXXX Bitter ('Fourex'). Queensland's detractors claim that this name was allocated because few Queenslanders could spell 'beer'. Numerous varieties of imported and 'boutique' beer are also available, and brew pubs flourish as palates become more adventurous and drinkers less conservative.

Bush Tucker

Early European pioneers learnt a lot about 'bush tucker' and bush medicine from the indigenous population, but their less adventurous countrymen who followed their trailblazing dismissed the millennium of local knowledge and forced European plants and animals on the land. Two centuries later, many lessons have been learnt, but droughts, weeds and erosion warn that Australians are still learning. Queensland's most celebrated bush food is the macadamia nut, also known as the Queensland nut, which was taken to Hawaii where it became a worldwide commercial success. You will not find many menus dominated by bush foods; however, you will find bush fruits, vegetables, herbs and spices flavouring many dishes in fine-dining restaurants. In Cairns, try Ochre Restaurant and Olivers for European flair utilising indigenous ingredients.

SHOPPING

With so much to see and do in Queensland's great outdoors you may be forgiven for leaving the shopping until some last-minute souvenir and gift purchasing. But the state's department stores, shopping strips, galleries and markets have plenty of bargains.

Sales

The major annual sales are after Christmas (from Boxing Day onwards) and at Easter and mid-year, in the lead-up to the end of the Australian financial year (30 June).

Opening Times

Most shops are open Mon–Fri 9am–5pm, with extended evening hours to 9pm on either or both Thursday and Friday. Saturday trading is usually 10am–5pm, while larger stores in big centres or tourist precincts will also trade on Sunday 10am–5pm.

Throughout Queensland there are ample opportunities to shop for everthing from boulder opals to raw cane sugar, and didgeridoos to surf gear. Some notable Australian manufacturers have outlets in key shopping and tourism centres. Among them is Akubra, whose famous broad-brimmed felt hats are characteristic of Australia. To complete the look, check out stockists of RM Williams, the brand named after the late and legendary bushman who designed and sold practical bushwear to rural Queenslanders for many years.

BRISBANE

Brisbane's Queen Street Mall, the centre of the city's shopping scene, offers more than 700 speciality shops spread across two city blocks. The blocks are dominated by two large department stores, Myers and David Jones, which sell pretty much everything at quite competitive prices. The pretty, heritage-listed Brisbane Arcade nearby showcases the work of Queensland's award-winning fashion designers.

A major shopping venue in Fortitude Valley is TCB Arcade, in the old TC Burns building fronting Brunswick Street Mall. Designer boutiques Gail Sorronda, Vein Wear and Subfusco are just a few of the outlets; parallel to the arcade runs Licorice Lane, lined with restaurants.

Some Aboriginal art is unique, and some is mass-produced. For the former try Footsteps Gallery, 166 Ann Street (tel: 3229 0395) in Brisbane, a respected showplace of Aboriginal and Torres Strait Islander art and artefacts.

South Bank comes alive with stalls at the weekend for the Lifestyle Markets (Fri 5–10pm, Sat 11am–5pm, Sun 9am–5pm), and on a Sunday morning, check out the Riverside Craft Market (8am–4pm) at Eagle Street Pier.

GOLD COAST

The Gold Coast features a number of huge shopping complexes, primary among them the Centro Surfers Paradise in Cavill Avenue. Other major consumer centres of note are The Oasis shopping centre, Victoria Avenue, Broadbeach, adjoining Conrad Jupiter's

Casino; Pacific Fair, Hooker Boulevard, Broadbeach; and Raptis Plaza, The Esplanade, Surfers Paradise (on the corner of Cavill Avenue).

The most reputable market on the Gold Coast is Carrara Markets (Sat–Sun 7am–4pm), which is located on the Nerang–Broadbeach Road near Pacific Fair. Aboriginal artefacts are also sold at the Kalwun Development souvenir shop, in the National Parks Information Centre (1171 Gold Coast Highway, Tallebudgera).

CAIRNS

The main shopping area in Cairns is the Central Business District, roughly bounded by the Esplanade, Shields, Spence and Grafton streets. There's a lot of variety, from fashion to souvenirs. The Esplanade Markets operate every Saturday (8am–4pm) at Fogarty Park and along the Esplanade. Further out of town, the Tjapukai Aboriginal Gallery (Kamerunga Road, Caravonica), adjacent to the Kuranda Skyrail terminal, is a showplace of authentic Aboriginal art and artefacts. Kuranda 'Original' Markets (5 Therwine Street; Wed–Fri, Sun 9am–4pm) make for a great shopping excursion from Cairns.

SUNSHINE COAST

All the produce sold at the thriving Noosa Farmers' Market (Weyba Road, Noosaville; Sun 7am–noon) is produced by the stallholders. About 15 minutes from Noosa, pretty Eumundi village draws throngs of tourists and locals to its twice-weekly markets (Wed 8am–1.30pm, Sat 6.30–2pm).

Above from far left: Queen Street Mall in Brisbane; sculptures by a local artist at Eumundi Markets.

Eat Queensland Queensland-produced foodstuffs are now very popular. These include macadamia nuts in various guises, tea and coffee from plantations in tropical north Queensland, koala-shaped pasta and, for adventurous carnivores, crocodile, shark or emu jerky.

Aboriginal Art

Aboriginal art is one of the most emblematic and evocative souvenirs of a visit to Australia. Aboriginal artists sell their work in community art centres, specialist galleries and through agents. Each artist owns the rights to his or her particular stories, motifs and tokens. Dot paintings from central Australia and bark paintings from northern Australia are the most common forms of Aboriginal art, but look out for contemporary works on canvas, board, boomerangs and didgeridoos, the Aboriginal musical instrument produced in northern Australia from tree branches hollowed out by termites. Boomerangs are always popular; genuine returning and hunting models usually come with instructions to help you throw them properly (and safely).

ENTERTAINMENT

Queensland's entertainment scene has blossomed visibly over recent years, and concerts, festivals and celebrations now punctuate the events calendar. Much of the activity is concentrated in Brisbane and the Gold Coast, but far north Queensland boasts numerous venues attracting events and talented acts.

What's on in Brisbane
To find out about cultural and entertainment events, check the useful listings website: www.brisbane247.com.

Queensland Notables
Queensland demonstrates a knack for producing internationally successful actors and rock bands. Diane Cilento, Billie Brown, Geoffrey Rush and Mount Isa-born Deborah Mailman have all achieved prominence. Home-grown pop bands include Savage Garden, Powderfinger, george, The Go Betweens and The Saints.

Thanks to a sunny outdoor lifestyle and the hero worship accorded sporting stars, the arts usually play second fiddle to sport. Nonetheless, Queensland has a lot to offer, thanks largely to the changes brought about by World Expo '88 and the development of the Queensland Cultural Precinct in Brisbane's South Bank. The Queensland Performing Arts Complex (QPAC) regularly hosts performers of international renown, and the state's capital is home to a fine symphony orchestra, an accomplished ballet, professional opera and theatre companies, as well as a full array of nightlife venues.

To complement – and to some extent challenge – mainstream cultural events, the city has nurtured alternative venues devoted to cutting-edge performances and exhibitions, notably the Brisbane Powerhouse and the Judith Wright Centre of Contemporary Arts. Inevitably, the primary cultural focus falls on Brisbane, but with more than 35 per cent of the state's population living in regional remote centres, touring has become an essential aspect of taxpayer-funded arts organisations. For more in-depth nightlife listings, *see pp.122–3*.

THEATRE

In Brisbane, it is entertaining to compare the delightfully old-fashioned Brisbane Arts Theatre (210 Petrie Terrace) with the stylishly grungy Brisbane Powerhouse (119 Lamington Street, New Farm) and the lively Judith Wright Centre of Contemporary Arts (420 Brunswick Street, Fortitude Valley). BAT, as the Arts Theatre is popularly known, has been churning out amateur drawing-room comedies, Agatha Christie-style mysteries, musical comedies and pantomimes since 1936. It's light years away from the Powerhouse, which operates within a once derelict building where graffiti and industrial machinery lend an edge to performance spaces mainly dedicated to the avant-garde *(see also p.122)*.

DANCE

Interestingly, the Queensland Ballet Company (www.queenslandballet.com.au) was not established with government patronage but by expatriate Frenchman Charles Lisner, who

danced with Edouard Borovansky's ballet company and the Royal Ballet in London before arriving in Brisbane in 1953 to found the Queensland Ballet, remaining at its helm until 1974. The company's major performances are staged at QPAC's Playhouse, but the thrice-annual Vis-à-Vis performances at the company's heritage-listed headquarters (424 Montague Road, West End; tel: 3013 6666) are a must if you are keen on dance.

MUSIC

The Queensland Orchestra (www.thequeenslandorchestra.com.au) delivers a programme of more than 70 concerts annually, from classics and new commissions to Baroque recitals at various venues in Brisbane. It also accompanies artists such as Nigel Kennedy, k.d. lang and Dionne Warwick. Brisbane also has a thriving jazz scene, partly centred on the Brisbane Jazz Club at Kangaroo Point, partly in Fortitude Valley bars such as Ric's Bar, The Press Club and The Bowery.

In Cairns, the Tanks Art Centre (www.tanksartcentre.com; 46 Collins Avenue, Edge Hill), out by the Botanic Gardens, is an eclectic venue featuring assorted musical acts.

NIGHTLIFE

The heart of Brisbane's nightlife is Fortitude Valley, which everybody calls 'The Valley', with one of Australia's best live music scenes. For up-to-date gig guides, consult the *Courier Mail* and the free *Time Off*, *Rave* and *Scene* magazines available at most music stores, pubs and clubs.

Around the Caxton Street/Petrie Terrace intersection precinct are several good venues. Leading the pack are: the Casablanca (tel: 3369 6969), a bar, café and steamy cellar club; the Hotel LA (tel: 3368 2560), a lively scene for under-35s; and The Bowery, 676 Ann Street (tel: 3252 0202), for a sophisticated locale and cocktails.

Above from far left: circus performers at the Woodford Folk Festival; the Lyric Theatre in the Queensland Performing Arts Complex.

Festivals

Brisbane's top festival is the Brisbane Festival (www.brisbanefestival.com.au), featuring a cultural and entertainment smorgasbord staged over three weeks in September. Brisbane Writers Festival (www.brisbanewritersfestival.com.au), also in September, brings renowned international authors to a city with a long literary pedigree of its own. The Brisbane Comedy Festival (www.briscomfest.com) in late February showcases established and up-and-coming Aussie talent and in May's Festival of Classics, hundreds of local classical musicians perform around Brisbane. The Brisbane Pride festival (www.pridebrisbane.org.au) celebrates gay and lesbian pride in June.

Outside Brisbane, the main events are the two-week Cairns Festival (www.festivalcairns.com.au) in August and the Woodford Folk Festival (www.woodfordfolkfestival.com), held at the end of December an hour's drive south of Noosa. The Dreaming Festival (www.thedreamingfestival.com), also at Woodford, in June, celebrates indigenous culture, music and dance.

SPORTS AND OUTDOOR ACTIVITIES

Queensland's legendary weather and pristine outdoors beckon all visitors to join in the fun, whether it is barracking for a football team, barrelling down a crystal-clear wave or floating around a coral garden surrounded by a swirling rainbow of fish.

Above from left: surfing at Caloundra; horse riding on the beach at Port Douglas; sea kayaking around Cairns.

This part of Australia is famous for its gruelling competitive spirit and robust partisanship when it comes to spectator sports such as football and cricket. The enthusiasm is infectious and, in comparison to the hooliganism witnessed elsewhere in the world, family-friendly. Queensland's hackneyed 'beautiful one day, perfect the next' mantra may have been discarded by the advertising agents, but the fact remains that the climate plus the coastline add up to an outdoor-activity mecca, whether it be a lazy round of golf, a challenging bushwalk or a lesson in surfing or scuba-diving.

SPECTATOR SPORTS

If you are keen to see one of the big football or cricket games, the ticket agency Ticketek (tel: 132849; www. ticketek.com.au) handles ticketing for most of the big games, or ask your travel agent prior to arrival.

There are four football codes played in Queensland: rugby league, rugby union, Australian rules and soccer. Rugby League is played by the National Rugby League (NRL; www. nrl.com.au) with two Queensland-based teams, the Brisbane Broncos and the North Queensland Cowboys. The biggest event in town, however, is when Queensland plays New South Wales in the State of Origin series – fiercely parochial matches with no

Learn to Surf

Queensland's surf beaches are concentrated in the southern corner of the state, where there's no Great Barrier Reef to interrupt the ocean swells. Surf schools have become something of a boom industry, with lots of newcomers entering the business. Surfing Australia runs coaching accreditation courses, and also accredits surf schools. Some unaccredited schools may still be excellent, and some accredited ones may not be. Generally, the schools run by former professional surfers offer very good services, and there is no denying the value of their years of experience. Some schools worth checking out: Cheyne Horan's School of Surf (Surfers Paradise; tel: 1800 227873; www.cheynehoran.com.au), Godfathers of the Ocean (Surfers Paradise; tel: 5593 5661; www.godfathersoftheocean) and Wave Sense (Noosa Heads; tel: 5474 9076; www.wavesense.com.au).

prisoners taken. Suncorp Stadium (tel: 3331 5000, www.suncorpstadium.com.au; Lang Park, Milton, Brisbane) hosts Queensland's rugby league, rugby union and soccer matches. The Gabba (tel: 3008 6166, www.thegabba.org.au; Vulture Street, Woolloongabba, Brisbane) is the home ground of the Brisbane Lions, Queensland's only AFL (Australian Football League) team. It also hosts major cricket matches.

OUTDOOR ACTIVITIES

Bushwalking

Visitors wanting to go bush while they are touring Queensland have plenty of opportunities. The Queensland government has progressively established walking tracks through some of the most beautiful parts of the state as part of its 'Great Walks' programme. More information about these walks is available from the Queensland Parks and Wildlife Service (www.epa.qld.gov.au). For further advice on bushwalking, see the Queensland Walks website (www.queenslandwalks.com.au).

Golf

Golf Queensland (www.golfqueensland.org.au) is a good starting point for golf players from abroad looking for information on public-access courses. Queensland has built a reputation for its golf-resort courses, with more than 10 on the Gold Coast and others on the Sunshine Coast and further north near the Whitsundays and Port Douglas.

Sailing and Sea Kayaking

Boating enthusiasts will find Queensland offers plenty of opportunities to indulge in their sport. Most are drawn to the 74 islands of the Whitsundays, where even novices are permitted to go 'bareboating', cruising the calm waters without any crew. There are dozens of operators hiring yachts, catamarans, tall ships and sea kayaks at Airlie Beach and Shute Harbour. To begin arranging boat charter before leaving home, see the Whitsunday Tourism website (www.tourismwhitsundays.com) or contact the Whitsunday Central Reservation Centre (tel: 4946 5299).

Snorkelling and Diving

Seeing the Great Barrier Reef up close through either diving or snorkelling is a must for any Queensland holidaymaker. Water temperatures stay warm all year round, and August through to January generally offer the best visibility. Scuba-diving in Queensland is highly organised, and you can trust any of the large number of established operators to deliver quality training, safety and a diver's certificate with loads of fun thrown in (see p.27). The minimum age for a course is 14 and you need to pass a non-strenuous medical examination.

Horse-Racing

The principal thoroughbred racing clubs in Queensland are the Queensland Turf Club (tel: 3268 2171; www.qtc.org), which races at Brisbane's Eagle Farm Racecourse (Lancaster Road, Ascot), and the Brisbane Turf Club (tel: 3268 6800; www.doomben.com), which races at Doomben Racecourse, Hampden Street, Ascot.

Cycling

As long as you avoid the humidity and downpours of the height of summer, cycling in Queensland is recommended. Bicycle Queensland (28 Vulture Street, West End; tel: 3844 1144; www.bq.org.au) has information on bicycle-user groups, cycle paths and ride programmes. The Transport Queensland website (www.transport.qld.gov.au/cycling) also carries information on cycle routes and maps published by local councils from the Gold Coast to Townsville.

GOLD COAST THEME PARKS

For adrenalin junkies, energetic teens or just the curious, the over-the-top theme parks of the Gold Coast have marvellous machines and water slides for gravity-propelled acceleration, providing all the exhilaration, glam, glitter and action to occupy a day or three.

Whatever your hobby or obsession, the Gold Coast probably offers it in the form of a 'world' or theme park. There's Bonsai World, Dreamworld, Frozen World, Sea World, Snooker World, Tropical Fruit World, Warner Brothers Movie World, Whitewater World and the World of Bees to mention just a few, all dishing up folly, fun, fear, fact, fantasy and fast food. Each of them is good value if its product is to your personal taste, or your children's.

The coast's most polished attractions are Sea World, Dreamworld, Whitewater World, Warner Brothers Movie World and Wet 'n' Wild Water World, all located 15 minutes' drive north of Surfers Paradise on the Gold Coast Highway.

SEA WORLD

Sea World (Seaworld Drive, Main Beach; tel: 5588 2222; www.seaworld. myfun.com.au; daily 10am–5.30pm) on the Southport Spit has developed its rides and performances in parallel with a programme of marine animal rescue

and welfare that caters for injured whales, dolphins, seals and sea lions.

Shark Bay comprises four large lagoons inhabited by various species of sharks. It is possible for visitors to scuba-dive and snorkel amongst the sharks and touch (very carefully) some of the smaller sea creatures. Another must-see is the Dolphin Cove Show, in which these perfectly trained sea mammals join equally well-rehearsed humans in a series of dazzling displays in the world's largest naturalistic lagoon habitat.

More unusually, Sea World also has a polar attraction – Polar Bear Shores – in an as-near-to-natural as possible Arctic summer environment, with wind generation, misting and fogging and rain simulation, as well as natural vegetation.

DREAMWORLD AND WHITEWATER WORLD

Ever wondered how it feels to fall backwards off a 38-storey building? Dreamworld (Dreamworld Parkway, Coomera; tel: 5588 1111; www.dream

Package Deals
The major theme parks offer various joint packages that provide discounted entry to two or more parks, so shop around. Note that last admission to attractions/rides is half an hour before the park closing times given here.

world.com.au; daily 10am–5pm, extended hours during school holidays) does a couple of pretty good simulations on its Tower of Terror. The park also offers a sliding scale of less alarming diversions, ranging from the Claw and the Wipeout to rides on rollercoasters, chairlifts, paddle steamers and trains. There is also an IMAX adventure theatre and native (and some international) wildlife, including dingoes, kangaroos and koalas.

Next door, and under the same management, is Whitewater World (Dreamworld Parkway, Coomera; www.whitewaterworld.com.au; daily 10am–4pm), featuring the massive funnel, the Green Room, various slides and tubes to ensure you get drenched, and a wave pool.

WARNER BROTHERS MOVIE WORLD

Warner Brothers Movie World (Pacific Motorway, Oxenford; tel: 5573 8485; www.movieworld.com.au; daily 10am–5.30pm) invites you to enjoy a well-presented, behind-the-scenes view of the illusions involved in movie-making. The latest attraction is Hollywood Stunt Driver, a simulation of an action movie set, in the best Hollywood tradition. It joins an old favourite, Shrek 4-D Adventure Show, with spectacular special effects, and some hair-raising rides, such as the Batwing Spaceshot and the Superman

Escape rollercoaster, where riders are hurled upwards at a speed of 100kph (60mph) and accelerate from 0–100kph in two seconds.

WET 'N' WILD WATER WORLD

Young kids and older thrill-seekers are well catered for at Wet 'n' Wild Water World (Pacific Motorway, Oxenford; tel: 5556 1650; www.wetnwildwaterworld.myfun.com.au; daily 10am–4pm, later in summer). Young children can head to Buccaneer Bay, while adrenalin junkies will love Extreme H_2O Zone with its huge slides and high-speed rides. Other highlights are the Giant Wave Pool and a 15-minute tube ride along a slow-moving river from the simulated tropical island's Calypso Beach.

Above from far left: rollercoaster at Dreamworld; Hollywood Stunt Driver at Warner Brothers Movie

Below: whirling through the 'Tornado' at Wet 'n' Wild Water World.

GREAT BARRIER REEF

The Great Barrier Reef, a protected World Heritage Area, is one of the most beautiful and diverse natural phenomena in the world, and its full wonder and glory are accessible to anyone who can don a mask and snorkel.

The Great Barrier Reef, one of the Seven Natural Wonders of the World, is an aquatic wilderness bigger than the UK, Holland and Switzerland put together. The reef extends over 250,000 sq km (96,500 sq miles) and comprises some 3,000 individual coral reefs and 940 islands running along the Queensland coast from north of Cape York Peninsula to just north of Fraser Island.

Declared a World Heritage Area in 1981, it is an extraordinarily complex ecosystem, a dazzlingly beautiful universe of low-wooded islands, mangrove estuaries, sea-grass beds, algae and sponge gardens, sandy and coral cays, mud floors and deep ocean troughs.

The largest structure built by living organisms on earth, the reef contains one-third of the known species of soft corals and more than 360 hard corals. It is also the home of 1,500 species of fish, dugongs, marine turtles, dolphins, whales, sea snakes, birds and sharks.

WHEN TO SEE THE REEF

Regardless of your reason for visiting the Great Barrier Reef, weather will play an important part in your enjoyment of its scenic attractions. From late April through to October it is at its best, the clear skies and moderate breezes offering perfect conditions for coral-viewing, diving, swimming, fishing and sunning. In November the first signs of the approaching 'Wet' appear: variable winds, increasing cloud and showers. By January it rains at least once most days. Even in the winter months, the water here is never cold, but it is worth paying a couple of dollars extra to hire a wetsuit anyway; most people find it hard not to go on snorkelling for hours in this extraordinary environment.

Below: reef sharks.

HOW TO SEE THE REEF

One of the easiest ways to visit the reef is to take a day trip from Cairns, Port Douglas, Airlie Beach and Cape Tribulation, among others. Almost all day trips follow a similar format: a morning dive, followed by a buffet lunch; then, assuming you have not eaten too much or partaken excessively of free beer, an afternoon dive. There should be a marine biologist on board, who will explain the reef's ecology. Before you book, also ask about the number of passengers the boat takes: this varies from several hundred to fewer than a dozen on smaller craft.

Learn to Dive

While snorkelling the reef satisfies many, you might want to learn to dive to maximise your experience. Recommended dive schools in Cairns include: Deep Sea Divers Den (tel: 4046 7333, www.diversden.com.au); Prodive Cairns (tel: 4031 5255, www.prodivecairns.com) and Tusa Dive (tel: 4047 9100, www.tusadive.com). For more, visit www.padi.com. These provide dive courses as well as organised dive trips (see p.23).

Day-Trip Operators

By no means a comprehensive list, the following operators run day trips to the reef. Great Adventures (Reef Fleet Terminal, 1 Spence Street, Cairns; tel: 1800 079080, 4044 9944; www.greatadventures.com.au) runs several options to Green Island, only 45 minutes from Cairns, as well as to a pontoon on the outer reef with semi-submersibles and underwater observatory. Also in Cairns, Reef Magic (Reef Fleet Terminal, 1 Spence Street; tel: 4031 1588; www.reefmagic.com.au) offers the chance to spend five hours at their Marine World pontoon moored at Moore Reef, with semi-submersible, optional guided snorkelling tours and helicopter flights.

The wave-piercing catamarans of Quicksilver Cruises based in Port Douglas (Marina Mirage; tel: 4087 2100; www.quicksilver.com.au) speed out to a floating platform at Agincourt Reef with an underwater observatory and semi-submersible vessel.

Cruises and Live-Aboard Vessels

Live-aboard vessels provide fully catered voyages where you overnight at sea to maximise the time spent on the reef. Voyages usually range from three to seven days, and the price includes all meals, entertainment and activities. Usually, but not exclusively, catering to experienced divers, live-aboard trips offer dive instructors and/or marine biologists along with the benefits of small-group touring. Operators include Coral Princess Cruises (tel: 4040 9999; www.coralprincess.com.au), which runs three- to seven-day cruises departing from Cairns and Townsville.

Above from far left: learning to dive; exploring the reef.

Reef Wrecks
The course of Australian history might have been very different had Commander James Cook been less fortunate when his ship *The Endeavour* ran aground on the reef in June 1770. By jettisoning a load of heavy cargo his crew managed to repair the ship and return to sea. Not all seafarers were so lucky; 30 shipwrecks lie in the reef's waters.

Sea Swimming

Ensure you swim only in designated waters; rip tides, box jellyfish and sharks mean that sea swimming, for example, off Fraser Island can be dangerous.

Great Barrier Reef Islands

Numerous continental islands and coral cays within the Great Barrier Reef region offer resort accommodation, from camping to luxury. The following is but a small selection of what is available:

Brampton Island (www.brampton-island.com). A lush, mountainous island in the southern Whitsundays with a romantic resort for couples, and an obvious absence of day-trippers and backpackers. Access by air or sea from Mackay.

Green Island (www.greenisland resort.com.au). A coral cay with eco-sensitive resort at the popular day-trip destination from Cairns.

Hamilton Island (www.hamilton island.com.au). The major resort island in the Whitsunday group, accessed from Airlie Beach, with numerous accommodation and tour options.

Heron Island (www.heronisland.com). Accessed via Gladstone, a coral cay with one boutique resort and miles and miles of coral reef.

Hook Island (www.hookislandresort. com). A wilderness island in the Whitsundays with one very basic 'resort' and several National Park campsites, offshore snorkelling and pristine beaches. Access is from Airlie Beach.

Lizard Island (www.lizardisland.com. au). A remote continental island, accessed by air from Cairns, with the famous Cod Hole, Osprey Reef and a five-star resort.

Below: accessing the reef by wave-piercing catamaran and sea plane.

Magnetic Island (www.magnetic-island.com.au). A delightfully unpretentious island, accessed by sea from Townsville, with several budget and mid-range accommodation and tour options.

Orpheus Island (www.orpheusisland. com). Out-of-the-way Orpheus is a luxurious retreat with just 21 communication-technology-free guest rooms. Access is by air from Townsville or Cairns.

Scenic Flights

Flying is an alternative way to experience the reef, where you may also spot migrating whales and sea turtles. Cairns Seaplanes (www.cairnssea planes.com) offers several tours combining a landing at Green Island and the chance to snorkel the reef.

EXPERIENCING THE REEF

Every morning dozens of state-of-the-art dive boats and wave-piercing catamarans head out from Cairns and Port Douglas to the outer reef. About an hour later, regardless of their departure point, they will be moored over the coral. Because the water is so shallow, snorkelling is perfectly satisfactory for experiencing the brilliant colours of the reef and marine life. Many people prefer it to the more technical scuba-diving; even so, most boats offer tanks for experienced divers and 'resort dives' for people who have never dived before.

As soon as you poke your head underwater, the world erupts. It's almost sensory overload: there are vast forests of staghorn coral, whose tips glow purple like electric Christmas-tree lights; brilliant-blue clumps of mushroom coral; layers of pink plate coral; and bulbous green brain coral. Tropical fish slip about, showing off their fluorescent patterns: painted flutemouth, long-finned batfish, crimson squirrel fish and hump-headed Maori wrasse. You should not interfere with any of the life on the reef, which is why buoyancy control is so important, and definitely do not touch a poisonous barbed stonefish or a conus textile shell; they shoot darts into anything that touches them, each with enough venom to kill 300 people!

As a general rule, the further out the boat heads, the more pristine the diving. But if a long voyage to the far reaches of the reef is a bit too daunting, rest assured you will still be amazed by the coral gardens and abundant marine life of the nearby reefs, which are cheaper to get to.

THREATS TO THE REEF

Of the many threats to the reef, the worst is coral bleaching. If the clear, tropical waters remain too warm for too long, corals expel their photosynthesising zooxanthellae and become colourless. Bleached corals are not necessarily dead and can regain their original algae if not too stressed, but if the water does not cool within about a month the coral will die.

Up to five percent of the Great Barrier Reef has been severely damaged during each of the last two major bleaching events, and increased temperatures from global warming are thought to be implicated.

Corals are also damaged by boat anchors, sewage from resorts, and by divers and snorkellers. The dugong and all six of the reef's marine turtle species are threatened because of the loss and degradation of their habitat, commercial and traditional fishing, and foxes taking their eggs on land.

When the Europeans settled, they cleared forests, mined, engaged in agriculture and established towns. Coastal wetland forest is still being cut down to make room for the beef cattle, sugar cane, cotton industries and banana plantations close to the coast. Hundreds of reefs are at risk from the sediment and chemical run-off from farming, and from the loss of the coastal wetlands that have acted as a natural filter in the past.

About a fifth of Queensland's population lives along the coast adjacent to the reef, and with the current inter-state and overseas migration to the state (over 200 people each day), communities continue to grow. How to manage water quality, tourism and commercial and recreational fishing is a major concern.

Above from far left: underwater scooters from the Great Adventures pontoon; snorkelling from the *Coral Princess*; Green Island.

Stingers
November to May is traditionally stinger (box jellyfish) season in North Queensland. Although not considered a great risk when swimming on the outer reefs, stingers are potentially deadly, and stinger suits can act as a preventative measure and also offer great protection from the sun. Stinger suits may be offered for purchase, hired or complimentary on board dive ships.

HISTORY: KEY DATES

Aborigines lived in Queensland for 50,000 years before the arrival of Captain Cook and the colonists who followed in his wake. An energetic population – explorers, emancipated convicts and free settlers – carved out a life in the hinterland. Today, the Gold Coast is the nation's fastest-growing region.

BEFORE THE EUROPEANS

c.50,000 BC   Ancestors of Aborigines arrive from eastern Asia via New Guinea when sea levels during the ice ages were low enough for the jouney to be made on foot.

THE FIRST EUROPEANS

1770   On 22 August Captain James Cook, aboard the *Endeavour*, raises the Union flag on Possession Island, Cape York, and claims eastern Australia for King George III.

1799   Explorer and navigator Matthew Flinders names Redcliffe Point, which becomes the site of Queensland's first European settlement.

1824   First convicts and jailers arrive at Redcliffe, on Moreton Bay. Country population (at time of European settlement) estimated at 300,000–500,000, at its densest along the north and east coasts.

1825   Convict settlement moved to present site of Brisbane's CBD.

1827   The rich pastoral country of the Darling Downs is discovered.

1831   Convict population peaks at 947.

1842   Brisbane is declared open for free settlement.

1846   Schooner *Coolangatta* wrecked. Brisbane becomes a port of entry.

1848   Queensland's first immigrant ship, *Artemisia*, reaches Moreton Bay.

STATEHOOD

1859   Statehood comes with separation from NSW and the naming of Queensland (European population 23,520).

1860s   Sugar planted at Redland Bay, providing a ready source of rum.

1875   Cobb & Co. initiates a stagecoach service linking Brisbane with Nerang Heads to the south.

1887	Brisbane connected by rail to Sydney. Difficulties (which still exist) arose because of Queensland's choice of narrow gauge which did not match that of the southern states.
1901	On 1 January Australia's six independent colonies are federated into the Commonwealth of Australia.

Above from far left: Brisbane harbour, 1891; the procession of the 41st Battalion through Brisbane on Anzac Day, 1916.

WAR AND PARADISE

1914	Australian troops leave home to join the allies in World War I.
1933	The Surfers Paradise township is named after hotelier James Cavill's hotel of the same name.
1939	Outbreak of World War II: Australian forces fight in Europe and the Middle East. Later in the war, Australia's military forces fight the Japanese in the Pacific theatre.
1941	First convoy of US servicemen arrives in Brisbane, which becomes a large military base.
1959	The city of Gold Coast established.
1974	Cyclone Wanda crosses the coast. Brisbane's worst flood since 1893.
1982	The 12th Commonwealth Games held in Brisbane.
1988	The nation celebrates its bicentenary. Brisbane hosts World Expo '88 with the Queensland-friendly theme 'Leisure in the Age of Technology'.
1992	Australian High Court rejects *Terra Nullus* (empty land) concept; theoretically great swathes of Crown Land could be claimed by Aboriginal groups under Native Title law.

21ST CENTURY

From 2000	Fed by immigration from the south, Queensland's population is growing at twice the national rate.
2002	Brisbane wins its second consecutive premiership in the national Australian Rules Football League.
2005	Brisbane launches its long-range bid for the 2024 Olympics.
2007	Brisbane's Gallery of Modern Art (GoMA), Australia's largest contemporary art space, opens its doors.
2009	The 150th anniversary of Queensland's proclamation as a separate colony commemorated with celebrations in Brisbane and regional centres.

Battle of Brisbane During World War II, Brisbane became a major base for Americans serving in the Pacific theatre, with General Douglas MacArthur directing the campaign from the AMP Building (now MacArthur Chambers) on Queen Street. One early and memorable conflict was a vigorous and physical exchange of views called 'the Battle of Brisbane', between the Americans and Australian soldiers, who cited three grievances against their allies; they were 'overpaid, oversexed and over here'.

WALKS AND TOURS

BRISBANE CITY CENTRE

This stroll around Brisbane's Central Business District (CBD) unveils Queensland's colonial history, showcases architectural landmarks, and taps into the bustle of one of Australia's fastest-growing cities. On the way, discover its wild and natural corners, shopping bazaars and dining scene.

DISTANCE 6km (3¾ miles)

TIME A half-day

START Riverside Centre

END Brisbane Arcade

POINTS TO NOTE

Let the weather influence your pace and timing on this walking tour and remember your sunscreen, hat and water. Along the way there are numerous places to buy a drink and catch breeze in the shade by the river. Although there is one hill, the steep climb comes early on in the tour, and overall it is not a particularly strenuous walk.

City Sights Tour
An excellent introduction to Brisbane is the City Sights bus tour (tel: 131230; www.citysights.com.au). Buses leave every 45 minutes from 19 stops, with the first bus leaving Post Office Square at 9am and the last bus departing from there at 3.45pm. There's informative commentary, and you can hop off and hop on a following bus to explore at your own pace. Your ticket permits same-day travel on CityCat ferry services.

As it meanders towards the coast, Queensland's longest river, the Brisbane, makes a deep loop around Spring Hill, which is the location of Brisbane's CBD at the heart of the city. This part of town lies about 20km (12 miles) upstream from where the river empties into Moreton Bay.

Historical Development

To the indigenous Yuggera people this mangrove-lined bend in the river was a traditional fishing ground and crossing point known as Min-an-jin.

The Moreton Bay penal settlement – the last major port to be established in the colony of what was then New South Wales – was founded in 1824 for the resettlement of repeat offenders from Sydney. Initially located at Redcliffe, the settlement was moved to North Quay, the site of the present CBD, in 1825 to improve security and gain access to a reliable supply of fresh water: the spring-fed creeks running off Spring Hill. In 1842 Britain closed the Moreton Bay penal settlement and declared the area open to free settlers. Private enterprise soon grasped the opportunities for growth, and the settlement's population grew to almost 6,000 by the time Queensland became a self-governing colony in 1859, with Brisbane anointed as its capital.

Today's bustling city barely has time to acknowledge its past, as new skyscrapers continue to vie for the title of Brisbane's tallest. Perhaps a late developer compared to its southern siblings, Brisbane shows no sign of slowing down or looking back.

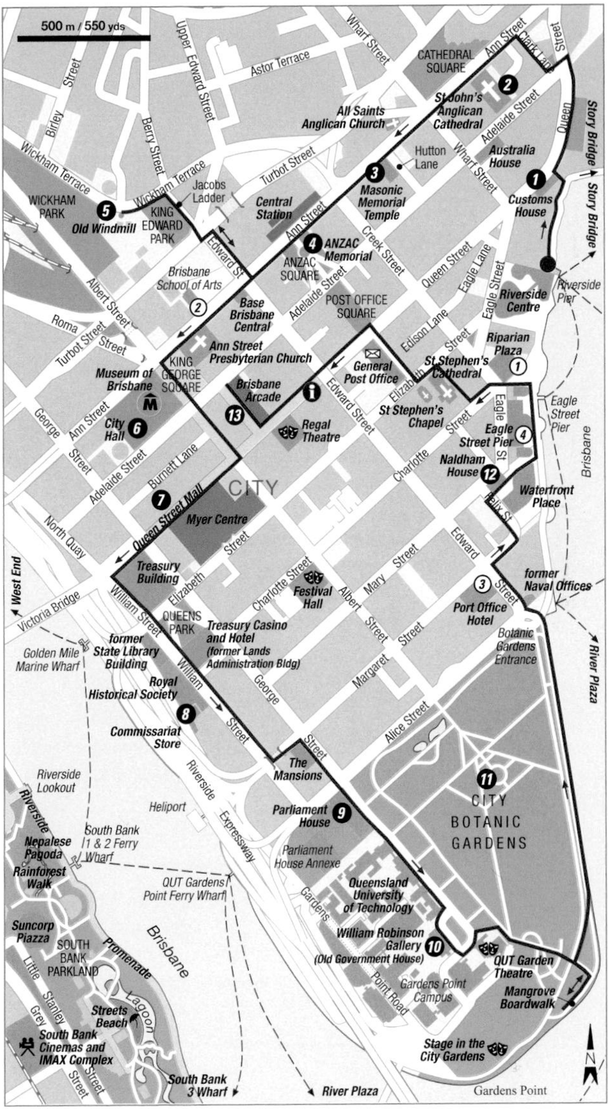

Above from far left: Story Bridge; George Street Mansions near Parliament House.

Public Transport

Translink (tel: 131230; www.translink.com.au) is responsible for bus, train and ferry transportation throughout Brisbane and southeast Queensland.

Below: the Commissariat Store houses a museum of the city's origins; Customs House.

Map labels

500 m / 550 yds

CATHEDRAL SQUARE
St John's Anglican Cathedral
All Saints Anglican Church
Adelaide Street
Australia House
Customs House
Story Bridge
Hutton Lane
Masonic Memorial Temple
Astor Terrace
Upper Edward Street
Wharf Street
Ann Street
Queen Street
Eagle Lane
Wickham Terrace
Birley Street
Berry Street
Turbot Street
WICKHAM PARK
Old Windmill
KING EDWARD PARK
Jacobs Ladder
Central Station
ANZAC Memorial
ANZAC SQUARE
Edward Street
Brisbane School of Arts
POST OFFICE SQUARE
Queen Street
Eagle Lane
Riverside Centre
Riverside Pier
Riparian Plaza
Albert Street
Roma Street
Turbot Street
Museum of Brisbane
KING GEORGE SQUARE
Ann Street Presbyterian Church
Base Brisbane Central
Brisbane Arcade
General Post Office
St Stephen's Cathedral
St Stephen's Chapel
Edison Lane
Eagle Street
Eagle Street Pier
Eagle St
City Hall
Regal Theatre
Charlotte Street
Eagle Street Pier
Naldham House
Waterfront Place
Burnett Lane
CITY
Adelaide Street
North Quay
Queen Street Mall
Myer Centre
Elizabeth Street
Charlotte Street
Festival Hall
Albert Street
Mary Street
Edward Street
former Naval Offices
Treasury Building
QUEENS PARK
Treasury Casino and Hotel (former Lands Administration Bldg)
George Street
Margaret Street
Port Office Hotel
Botanic Gardens Entrance
River Plaza
West End
Victoria Bridge
Golden Mile Marine Wharf
former State Library Building
Royal Historical Society
William Street
Commissariat Store
Riverside
Alice Street
CITY BOTANIC GARDENS
Riverside Lookout
South Bank 1 & 2 Ferry Wharf
Heliport
The Mansions
Parliament House
Parliament House Annexe
Nepalese Pagoda
Rainforest Walk
QUT Gardens Point Ferry Wharf
Queensland University of Technology
Suncorp Piazza
SOUTH BANK PARKLAND
Promenade
Brisbane
William Robinson Gallery (Old Government House)
QUT Garden Theatre
Mangrove Boardwalk
Streets Beach
South Bank Cinemas and IMAX Complex
Gardens Point Campus
Point Road
Stanley Street
Little Stanley Street
Lagoon
South Bank 3 Wharf
River Plaza
Stage in the City Gardens
Gardens Point

Bridge-Climbing

Look for climbers on the top girders of Story Bridge. If you would like to join them, check out Story Bridge Adventure Climb (www.story bridgeadventureclimb. com.au).

BRISBANE RIVER

Start amidst the architecturally acclaimed high-rise **Riverside Centre** and **Riparian Plaza** which dominate the **Riverside Precinct**. Have breakfast at the **Boardwalk Bar & Bistro**, see ⑪①, where you can watch the CityCat ferries beetle under Story Bridge *(see margin left and p.38)* to disgorge well-dressed commuters at the pier.

Customs House

Head north (downstream) along the Riverside Promenade and after a few hundred metres the stately, copper-domed **Customs House ❶** comes into view. This colonnaded example of Victorian architecture was constructed in 1886–9; it is now owned by the University of Queensland and provides an interesting visual contrast to the glass skyscrapers towering behind. Climb the well-worn sandstone stairs and skirt around the northern side of the building, to emerge on Queen Street. The impressive 1888 facade opposite is the remnant of a warehouse, indicating, along with Customs House, the significance of river trade during the boom-time of the late 1800s.

Turn right and walk along Queen Street to the intersection with Adelaide Street; the small park on your right next to the Brisbane Marriott Hotel affords more views of the river. Cross Adelaide Street and ascend the narrow Clark Lane to Ann Street and turn left.

ST JOHN'S CATHEDRAL

Ann Street boasts several significant religious buildings, but taking pride of place is the Gothic Revival **St John's Anglican Cathedral ❷** with its soaring steeple at no. 373. The foundation stone was laid in 1901, but construction continued on and off for over 100 years. Architecture buffs will be excited by Australia's only example of a vaulted ceiling constructed entirely of stone.

Continue southwest down Ann Street. Just past Hutton Lane is the impressive facade of the **Masonic Memorial Temple ❸** (no. 311; tel: 329 3533; tours Mon–Fri 2pm; free) with its four-storey-high columns. Built in 1930, the temple has a striking Grand Hall and Grand Foyer.

ANZAC SQUARE

Keep walking downhill along Ann Street and cross over Creek Street. The clock tower of **Central Station** is soon on your right, and directly opposite is the poignant **Anzac Square War Memorial and Parkland ❹**. The **Shrine of Remembrance** features an eternal flame and 18 columns representing 1918, the year that peace was declared after World War I. Beneath is an underpass to Central Station and a **World War II Shrine of Memories** (Mon–Fri 9am–2.15pm; free).

Cross over Ann Street to Central Station, and continue towards the

Edward Street intersection. On the corner diagonally opposite is the elaborate Base Brisbane Central hostel building, which was built for the Salvation Army in 1911.

KING EDWARD PARK

Turn right at Edward Street, and climb the hill to cross over Turbot Street and enter **King Edward Park**. The entrance to the park is guarded by three striking bronze sculptures looking like props from a sci-fi movie. Panels reveal they are actually sets from a classical play, *Agamemnon*. Behind the sculptures, the bright red steps of Jacobs Ladder lead you towards **Spring Hill** and the high point of this walk. Turn left at the top of the stairs and head towards the **Old Windmill** ❺. Established in 1828, this modest structure is Queensland's oldest surviving building. Its dubious effectiveness as a windmill led to it becoming powered by a treadmill and thus a device for punishing unruly convicts. Return to Edward Street, and turn right along Ann Street.

KING GEORGE SQUARE

About 50m/yds from the corner is **Bleeding Heart**, see ①②, a breakfast, lunch and coffee stop set in the Brisbane School of Arts building. Continue along Ann Street until you reach **King George Square**, where **Brisbane City Hall** ❻ dominates this expansive public space. City Hall hosts the **Museum of Brisbane** (tel: 3403 4048; www.museumofbrisbane.com.au; daily 10am–5pm; free), displaying the history of Brisbane as well as contemporary art. Note that during renovations (due to be finished in 2012), the museum will occupy 157 Ann Street. Take a lift up City Hall's bell tower for stupendous views; afterwards, stroll south through the square to cross Adelaide Street and walk one block down Albert Street.

The shopping precinct of **Queen Street Mall** ❼ is pedestrianised between Edward and George streets and hosts a multitude of shopping and eating possibilities *(see also p.39)*. For now, continue towards George Street and cross over towards the Treasury Building.

(see also p.39)

Above from far left: Shrine of Remembrance in Anzac Square; pediment of Brisbane City Hall; Old Windmill.

Food and Drink

① BOARDWALK BAR & BISTRO
Riparian Plaza, 71 Eagle Street; tel: 3221 0026; www.boardwalkbar.com.au; daily 7.30am–late; $$
With sail-shaded tables right on the boardwalk, this is riverside dining at its best. Watch the city wake up as the sun rises over Kangaroo Point while you energise over a breakfast of fresh juice, espresso coffee, toasted muesli with fruit compote and yoghurt, corn fritters, or eggs and bacon.

② BLEEDING HEART
166 Ann Street; tel: 3229 0395; www.bleedingheart.com.au; Mon–Fri 6.30am–4.30pm; $$
The deep and beautiful verandas of the sandstone School of Arts building shelter this charming gallery and café with fairtrade coffee and tea and refreshing ice-cream sodas. Try the ginger beer ice-cream soda while relaxing on the elevated veranda.

WILLIAM STREET

Continue west alongside the Italianate **Treasury Building**, which houses the 24-hour casino behind its numerous arches, and turn left down William Street. Stroll through Queens Park with its stern statue of Queen Victoria and pass by the grand **Lands Administration Building**, now the Treasury Casino and Hotel *(see p.112)*. On the opposite side of the road is the **Commissariat Store ❽** (no. 115; tel: 3228 4198; Tue–Fri 10am–4pm; free), an 1829 convict-era building housing a museum focusing on Brisbane's earliest beginnings and local Aboriginal history.

PARLIAMENT HOUSE

Cross back to the eastern side of William Street and head south to Margaret Street and turn left. Turn right on George Street passing **The Mansions**, charming three-storey terraced housing, on the way to **Parliament House ❾** (corner George and Alice streets; www.parliament.qld.gov.au; Mon–Fri 9am–4.30, Sat–Sun 10am–2pm; free), where there are on-demand guided tours of the fully restored interior and decorative antiques. Alternatively, catch all the action or boredom from the visitors' gallery when parliament sits *(see website)*.

Resume your walk south past the lush Botanic Gardens on your left and the Queensland University of Technology (QUT) on your right. Soon a sweeping

driveway on your right heralds the presence of the serene, creamy-stone **Old Government House ❿** (2 George Street; tel: 3138 8005; www.ogh.qut.edu.au; Sun–Fri 10am–5pm; free). Once the home of Queensland's governors, the attractive mansion also houses the exceptional **William Robinson Gallery**, filled with the work of this award-winning Queensland artist.

CITY BOTANIC GARDENS

Cross over George Street, past the QUT Gardens Theatre and enter the **City Botanic Gardens ⓫** (daily, 24 hours; free; for cycle hire, *see margin p.40*). Originally a convict-worked farm, the gardens were formally laid out in 1855. Consider pausing at the café for refreshments, then head down the stone steps through rainforest towards the river. At the Riverside Promenade, turn right where you will see a boardwalk extending out into the **mangrove forest**. Follow the boardwalk looking for birdlife and read about the significance of the muddy mangrove ecosystem on panels. Rejoin the promenade and head north.

EDWARD STREET TO EAGLE STREET

Exit the gardens at Edward Street passing the erstwhile **Naval Offices**, now occupied by upmarket boutiques and restaurants, on your right. On the

Above: mangrove boardwalk; Botanic Gardens sculpture.

Story Bridge Hotel
Looking for a detour? From the Eagle Street Pier hop on a stubby river ferry heading to Holman Street on Kangaroo Point. The ferry ride affords great views of the city and Story Bridge, particularly at night. Turn right outside the Holman Street terminal and follow the riverside walkway for 500m/yds as far as Bright Street. Turn left and you will spot the renowned Story Bridge Hotel tucked under the Story Bridge approach ramp. There are drinking and dining options from rowdy to relaxing in this atmospheric watering hole *(see p.122)*.

corner with Margaret Street is the **Port Office Hotel**, see ⑪③, a popular lunch option. Turn right at Margaret Street and then left along Felix Street. At the Mary Street intersection, turn right beside the colonial **Naldham House** ⑫. When you reach the anchor beside the eastern wall, turn around. Three small brass plaques on the corner of the building mark the water levels of the 1893, 1896 and 1974 floods. Can't see the 1893 plaque? Look up!

Pass under the shade sails towards the river and the **Eagle Street Pier** complex. Here are more eateries and cafés – **Cha Cha Char Wine Bar and Grill**, see ⑪④, is a favourite haunt of carnivorous locals with its mouth-watering steaks – paddle-steamer cruise boats (tel: 3221 1300; www.kookaburrariverqueens.com) and a ferry terminal. Catch a ferry here to Holman Street for the Story Bridge Hotel *(see margin, opposite)*.

BACK TO QUEEN STREET MALL

Head west, away from the river to the intersection of Creek, Eagle and Charlotte streets. Walk southwest along Charlotte Street towards the steps leading up to the beautifully refurbished **St Stephen's Cathedral** (entrance on Elizabeth Street) dating from the 1860s, and the neighbouring **St Stephen's Chapel**, Queensland's first church, built in 1850.

Cross Elizabeth Street in front of the cathedral and take the narrow lane between Brisbane GPO and Newspaper House to emerge on Queen Street with the open plaza of **Post Office Square** opposite. Turn left on Queen Street and cross over Edward Street to enter Queen Street Mall. Pass by the helpful **Brisbane Visitor Information Centre** (Queen Street Mall; tel: 3006 6290; www.visitbrisbane.com.au; daily 9am–5pm) and walk 400m/yds until you reach **Brisbane Arcade** ⑬ on your right. The three storeys of the arcade, which runs through to Adelaide Street, are crammed with tempting elegant tearooms, jewellers and high-end fashion shops.

Above from far left: elegant Brisbane Arcade; Old Government House.

Brisbane 5 in 1
This gives the purchaser the chance to choose five of 12 possible experiences and attractions, and receive a discount on the full purchase price. See www.brisbane5in1card.com.au.

Food and Drink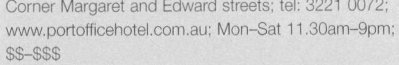

③ PORT OFFICE HOTEL
Corner Margaret and Edward streets; tel: 3221 0072; www.portofficehotel.com.au; Mon–Sat 11.30am–9pm; $$–$$$
Choose between a good-value bar meal in the casual Marble Bar, tapas in the Fix Bar or elegant dining in the Fix Restaurant. There are wood-fired pizzas, vegetarian dishes and seafood, though the steaks from the grill enjoy pride of place on the menu.

④ CHA CHA CHAR WINE BAR AND GRILL
Shop 5 Plaza Level, Eagle Street Pier; tel: 3211 9944; www.chachachar.com.au; Mon–Fri noon–11pm, Sat–Sun 6–11pm; $$$
If you still have not succumbed to Queensland's obsession with succulent steaks, here is the place to give in to temptation. The menu will make you an instant expert in all things steaky. Digest the facts about breeding, feed, location and age before devouring the subject. Booking is recommended.

BRISBANE SOUTH BANK

Filled with entertainment and dining options and wrapped in green parklands, South Bank is Brisbane's playground and Queensland's premier cultural precinct: the area is designed just as much for strolls and relaxation as it is for showcasing its various edifying and recreational attractions.

Pedal to South Bank and Beyond
Just inside the Albert Street entrance to the City Botanic Gardens is a gaggle of bikes belonging to Valet Cycle Hire (tel: 0408 003198). Brisbane has hundreds of kilometres of cycle paths, and Valet has plenty of bikes and suggested riverside routes to keep you pedalling. They will even deliver a bike to your hotel.

DISTANCE 3.75km (2½ miles) walk; 5km (3-mile) CityCat ride
TIME A leisurely full day
START Goodwill Bridge
END South Bank Wharf 1
POINTS TO NOTE
This walk starts on the CBD side of the Brisbane River, near the City Botanic Gardens, and crosses the river on the car-free Goodwill Bridge. You can return to the CBD by either this or the solar-powered Kurilpa footbridge, or by Victoria Bridge, but the CityCat (tel: 131230; www.translink.com.au/ ferries) affords a more relaxing return trip with great views, and delivers you to the Riverside Precinct, yet another locality crammed with dining options (see p.36).

South Bank was developed for the 1988 World Expo, and as such it is an outstanding example of the positive legacy such large public events can bestow on cities. This former industrial wasteland now has something for everyone: bring your bathers for a splash at Streets Beach, your head for heights for a spin on the Wheel of Brisbane, and your sense of adventure for the Gallery of Modern Art.

Begin at the **Goodwill Bridge ❶** on Gardens Point near the southwest corner of the City Botanic Gardens *(see p.38)*, close to the outdoor **River Stage**. Built in 2001, this bridge takes its name from Brisbane's Goodwill Games held in the same year. A small coffee stand, serving good espresso, is parked on the bridge towards this end.

QUEENSLAND MARITIME MUSEUM

At the other end of the bridge, a tugboat, a warship and a very odd-looking lightship (half-lighthouse, half-ship) announce the **Queensland Maritime Museum ❷** (Stanley Street; tel: 3844 5361; www.maritimemuseum.com.au; daily 9.30am–4.30pm, last entry at 3.30pm; charge). Since Dutch explorers landed on Cape York Peninsula in 1606, the sea has shaped Queenslanders' lives and commerce, and this museum focuses on the state's close links with the sea and historical dependence on it.

SOUTH BANK PARKLANDS

Opposite the museum you will see the entrance to the **Arbour**, a bougainvillea-draped archway of metal tendrils and wire supports. This living art form shelters a path that meanders through the South Bank Parklands as far as the Wheel of Brisbane (see p.42).

Heading northwest along the Arbour you pass between shady picnic grounds and The Boardwalk, the first of The Arbour's several restaurant zones (closed for renovations at the time of writing). A small formal garden appears on your right with a statue of Confucius, where the Arbour swings around a cluster of cafés.

Stanley Street Plaza

Where the cafés end, the **Stanley Street Plaza ❸** begins. A usually quiet public space featuring the **South Bank Visitor Centre** (South Bank House, Stanley Street Plaza; tel: 3867 2051; daily 9am–5pm), the plaza comes alive with buskers and market-goers at the weekend as the venue for the **Lifestyle Markets** (Fri 5–10pm, Sat 10am–5pm, Sun 9am–5pm). Stalls sell all manner of items, from chilli sauces and sarongs to sombreros and temporary tattoos.

Little Stanley Street

Parallel to the plaza and bordering the parklands, Little Stanley Street is packed with bars and quality restaurants offering casual sidewalk dining. Even if you are not yet hungry, check out what's on offer for future reference. The range of cuisine served up is extraordinary, and includes the exotic ambience and Turkish cuisine of **Ahmet's**, see ⑪①, and the modern Asian flavours of **Obsession Restaurant**, see ⑪②.

Streets Beach

Between Stanley Street Plaza and the river is **Streets Beach ❹** (daily, free), Australia's only city-bound beach. This man-made lagoon complete with sandy shore and lifesavers is a surreal sight with a muddy river and city skyline as a backdrop, but with no waves and dangerous rips and plenty of shady palm trees, it is one of South Bank's most popular attractions.

Above from far left:
cycling on the South Bank; Streets Beach.

Food and Drink

① AHMET'S
10/164 Grey Street; tel: 3846 6699; www.ahmets.com; daily 11.30am–3pm, Sun–Thur 5–9pm, Fri–Sat 5–10pm; $$
Be transported to a vibrant bazaar in this colourfully atmospheric Turkish restaurant. Attention to detail extends to the dishes, best shared, which are simply delicious. Dive into the dips, but leave room for the spicy lamb *pide* or the delicious *guvec* (casserole) made with lamb, chicken or vegetables. Entry is from both Grey and Little Stanley streets.

② OBSESSION RESTAURANT
5 Little Stanley Street; tel: 3844 3373; www.obsession chinese.com.au; Mon 11am–3pm, Sun–Thur 11am–3pm & 5–10pm, Fri–Sat 11am–3pm & 5–11pm; $$$
Delicate Chinese and Southeast Asian specialities, such as Singapore-style chilli bugs and *ma po* tofu, are prepared with organic and free-range produce in a chic setting with indoor and pavement seating.

Check out www.
visitsouthbank.com.
au for an events
calendar and detailed
information on all
attractions.

Below: Queensland
Performing Arts
Centre; sculpture
in front of the
State Library.

Rainforest Walk

North of the beach, the Arbour weaves
between clusters of cafés and restaurants and the Suncorp Piazza, a
well-used concert venue that often
also screens sport or movies free. Take
the **Rainforest Walk**, where you
should spot a water dragon, a striking
yet harmless lizard. The boardwalk
emerges at the intricately carved
Nepalese Pagoda, constructed for the
1988 World Expo.

Wheel of Brisbane

Towering almost 60m (197ft) above the
parklands, the **Wheel of Brisbane** ❺
(www.thewheelofbrisbane.com.au;
charge) is worth a spin. You receive geo-
graphical and historical commentary
while inside your air-conditioned pod.

QUEENSLAND
CULTURAL CENTRE

Much of Queensland's celebration of
culture culminates in this assemblage
of edifices at the northern end of the
South Bank Parklands. As you leave
the Wheel of Brisbane, walk north
along the Cultural Forecourt. On your
left is the **Queensland Performing
Arts Centre (QPAC)** ❻ (corner Grey
and Melbourne streets; tel: 3840 7444;
www.qpac.com.au). With several
theatres, galleries and event spaces,
there is usually something on.

Turn left to skirt the northern side of
QPAC where there are lifts and stairs
that lead to a walkway over Melbourne
Street and the **Queensland Museum**
❼ (corner Grey and Melbourne streets;
tel: 3840 7555; www.southbank.qm.
qld.gov.au; daily 9.30am–5pm; free).
This compact, well-laid-out museum
succinctly explores Queensland's natural and social history. The Museum
Zoo is a creative line-up of stuffed critters where you can compare your own
size and physical abilities against
members of the animal kingdom.
There is also a kid-friendly, hands-on
Sciencentre (charge).

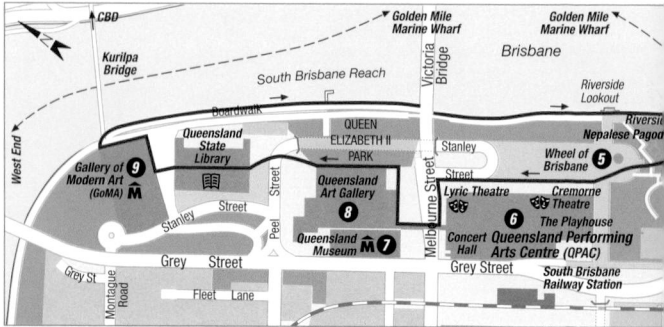

Two Galleries

Exit the museum where you entered. On your left, the **Whale Mall** reverberates to the recordings of humpback whales. Look up to see life-size recreations of these mammals. Straight ahead is a passage heading towards the river and the **Queensland Art Gallery** ❶ (Stanley Place; tel: 3840 7303; www.qag.qld.gov.au; Mon–Fri 10am–5pm, Sat–Sun 9am–5pm; free). Head along the passage and find the entrance on the river side of the gallery. Inside, visiting exhibitions accompany indigenous, classical and contemporary art from Australia and abroad, particularly Asia and the Pacific.

Exit the gallery from the northern side and walk across the elevated plaza towards the **Queensland State Library** (www.slq.qld.gov.au; daily 10am–5pm, to 8pm Mon–Thur). Pass through the centre of the library via the Knowledge Walk *(see margin, right)*. This ground-floor walkway opens out onto a compound facing the dramatic, glass and steel **Gallery of Modern Art (GoMA)** ❾ (Stanley Place; same contact details as the Queensland Art Gallery; free). The light-filled modern space showcases contemporary art in a variety of media.

KURILPA BRIDGE TO SOUTH BANK WHARF 1

Northeast of GoMA, a lawn descends to the Riverside Boardwalk. To the north, **Kurilpa Bridge**, a sculptural (and controversial) structure of steel masts and cables, with solar-powered LED lighting, is a bridge for pedestrians and cyclists thats connects South Bank with the CBD. If your accommodation is in the north of the city this would be the quick way back to base. Otherwise, turn south and follow the boardwalk under Victoria Bridge back to **South Bank Wharf 1**. Here you can catch a CityCat ferry and cruise past Gardens Point to the Riverside Centre.

Above from far left:
Queensland State Library; Kurilpa Bridge.

South Bank Online
Bring your charged up laptop for free WiFi at the State Library of Queensland. Travellers congregate within the sheltered Knowledge Walk to get online.

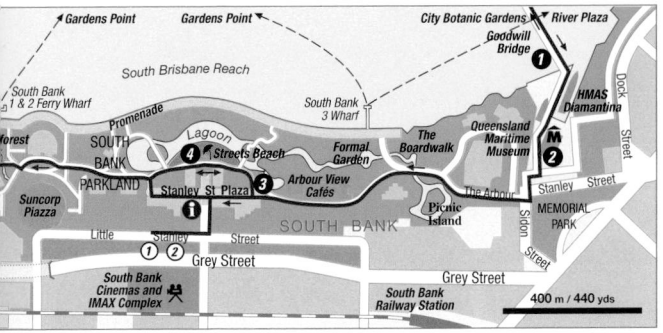

MORETON ISLAND

Moreton Island, just a short ferry trip from Brisbane, delivers a great action-packed day. Four-wheel driving along its vast sandy beaches, plunging into a pristine blue lagoon, snorkelling among shipwrecks, and hand-feeding wild dolphins are just part of what's on offer.

DISTANCE 50km (31 miles)

TIME A full day

START/END Tangalooma Island Resort

POINTS TO NOTE

You will need a 4WD vehicle for this trip, either hired in Brisbane *(see p.108)* or pre-booked from Tangalooma Resort *(see opposite)*. The Tangalooma Launch departs at 7.30am and 10am from Pinkenba Wharf, Holt Street, Pinkenba (arrive 30 min early). The resort also offers coach transfers (charge) from city hotels for the 10am launch. Vehicles take the MiCat vehicle barge (14 Howard Smith Drive; tel: 3909 3333; www.moretonventure.com; Mon and Wed–Sun 8.30am) from the Port of Brisbane. You will need a vehicle access permit (charge), obtained from the MiCat barge or from the Environmental Protection Agency (tel: 131304; www.derm. qld.gov.au/parks/). Bring a picnic lunch or eat in the resort. For accommodation, book ahead at Tangalooma Resort *(see p.112)*.

Organised Island Tours

As an alternative to driving your own 4WD, try a guided day tour. The many operators that offer these from Brisbane include Goanna Adventures (tel: 3841 7781; www.goanna adventures.com.au) and Sunrover Expeditions (tel: 1800 353 717; www. sunrover.com.au). Alternatively, take the Tangalooma Launch and book a Tangalooma Resort tour (tel: 3410 6000; www. tangalooma.com).

Until the early 1960s, visitors crossed Moreton Bay to Tangalooma on Moreton Island to witness the gruesome spectacle of whales being butchered for processing into products such as edible oils, whalebone garments and livestock food. The site was one of the world's largest whaling stations, operating from 1951 to 1962, conveniently located close to a narrow deep-water channel, along which about 10,000 humpback whales migrated every year. It was estimated that just 500 humpbacks remained ten years after the whaling station was established. Soon after, the authorities put a stop to all whaling from Tangalooma.

Today, Moreton Island is over 95 percent National Park, and is home to just three small villages and Tangalooma Island Resort. The latter now occupies the whaling station site; indeed whales are still among Tangalooma's main attractions. Between June and November, when the humpbacks perform spectacular tail and flipper slapping and giant breaches, there are whale-watching cruises on offer which you can combine with your Tangalooma Launch voyage.

TANGALOOMA ISLAND RESORT

Tangalooma Island Resort ❶ (tel: 3410 6000; www.tangaloma.com) offers several dining options, a general store, an ATM and numerous land- and water-based activities, as well as accommodation. Unless you have driven to the island, this is where you will pick up your pre-booked 4WD. Before you head off, grab a snack and drink from the **Beach Café**, see 🍴① *(p.47)*.

Follow signs to the track that leads onto the beach (there is a no-driving zone in front of the resort): the drive will now be entirely on sand. Note that the best and safest time for beach driving is two hours either side of low tide; tide charts are provided with the

Above: Tangalooma Island Resort.

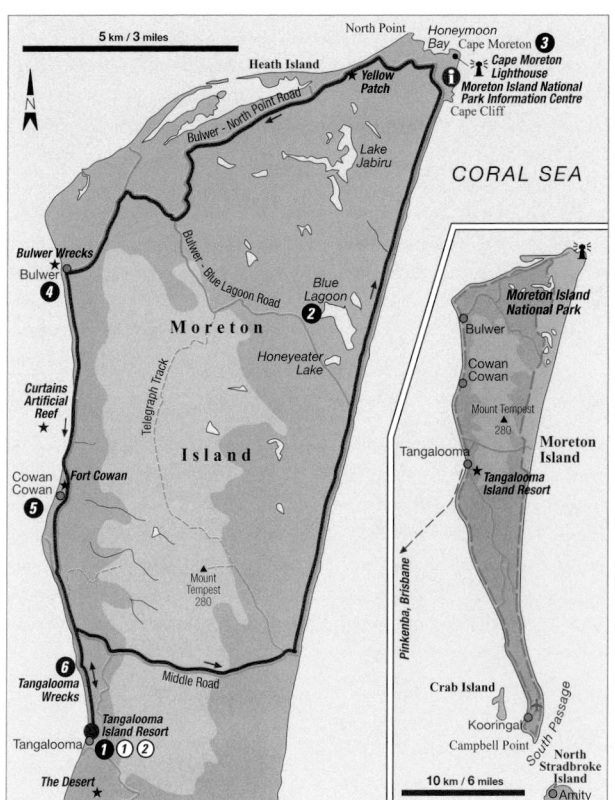

Above: feeding the local pelicans; idyllic beach view.

Snorkelling

A guided snorkelling trip is the best way to experience the colourful marine life around the Tanga-looma Wrecks. Tangalooma Resort's Dive In Sports (tel: 3410 6924; daily 8am–5pm) offers one guided snorkel per day, usually on high tide. Snorkelling gear and wetsuits are provided.

island driving permit or the resort vehicle hire. The tour, with stops, will take approximately four hours. To start, head north just past the **Tangalooma Wrecks** *(see opposite)*, and take the inland track, Middle Road.

BLUE LAGOON

After 7km (4 miles) you will reach the eastern side of the island. Turn left and head north along this beautiful 38km (24-mile) stretch of ocean beach. After 8km (5 miles), leave the beach to visit the **Blue Lagoon ❷**, the island's largest freshwater lake, with white sandy shores lapped by clear-blue water. It is a short stroll from the parking area through heathland down to the lake. The sand may be hot on bare feet but it just makes a swim here even more inviting.

Bottlenose Dolphins

Moreton Bay is home to approximately 600 bottlenose dolphins and just on sunset Tangalooma is visited by a small pod, normally up to 11 dolphins, which frequent the shores to feed, hunt and play. You are encouraged to learn and identify these endearing creatures by their individual and quite distinctive dorsal fin markings. Anyone can join on the jetty to watch this nightly spectacle; however, if you wish to join in the hand-feeding you must be an overnight guest at the resort or be booked on the resort's extended day tour with dolphin-feeding. And you will also need to register at the resort's Marine Education and Conservation Centre from 1–5pm.

CAPE MORETON

A further 8km (5 miles) north is the tip of **Cape Moreton ❸**, where stunning 360-degree views stretch to the Glass House Mountains *(see p.49)* on the mainland and to North Stradbroke Island *(see p.52)*. You can sit and watch marine wildlife below as you have a picnic lunch: turtles, dolphins, sharks, whales, rays and schools of fish are commonly spotted.

The 1.5km (1-mile) walk around the headland (the only part of the island that is not pure sand) winds past the 23m (115ft) -high **Cape Moreton Lighthouse**, the oldest operating lighthouse in Queensland and an important navigation aid to all ships entering the Bay. It was built in 1857 with sandstone blocks quarried by 35 prisoners. The unmanned **Moreton Island National Park Information Centre** near the lighthouse provides island history and details on marine life and island wildlife.

Return to the car park and continue west on the inland track, which briefly returns to the beach past **Yellow Patch**, a large dark-yellow sand blow (drifting dunes created when denuded of vegetation). The track then veers inland once again to bypass several tidal lagoons.

BULWER AND COWAN COWAN

Back on the western side of the island, the route passes behind the tiny settle-

ments of Bulwer and Cowan Cowan. (The beaches in front of these two small communities are closed to traffic.)

On the beach at **Bulwer ❹**, three hulks lie on the sand, having been originally scuttled and placed there in the 1930s to form a safe anchorage for small boats. Some 5.5km (3½ miles) further south, **Cowan Cowan ❺** is the site of Fort Cowan, an old navy signal station that was Brisbane's first line of defence during World War II.

TANGALOOMA WRECKS

It is only a short drive now along the beach to one of the island's most recognisable landmarks – the **Tangalooma Wrecks ❻**. In total, 15 former hard-working ships that once sailed all around Australia have been scuttled here to form a small-craft anchorage. *The Maryborough*, an iron-hulled bucket dredge built in 1885, was the first to be scuttled in July 1963. The wrecks are perfect for snorkelling *(see margin, opposite)* and scuba-diving.

TANGALOOMA ACTIVITIES

It is now time to return to **Tangalooma Island Resort**, where thrill-seekers can chose from a range of afternoon activities, including quadbike rides in the dunes, jet ski rides, parasailing and seasonal whale-watching cruises. The **Desert Safari**

Tour (four daily, 1½ hours duration; charge) includes a 4WD bus tour through the bush to 'the desert'. This is in fact a 42ha (100-acre) sandblow. The huge dunes are the venue for **sand tobogganing**; a flimsy piece of waxed board is all you need to fly down at exhilarating speeds of about 60kph (40mph). There is nothing to fear, except a mouthful of sand if you do not follow instructions correctly.

After all that you might want some sustenance. Along with the licensed **Beach Café**, see ⑪①, the resort has a couple of good (seasonal) restaurants including the **Steakhouse**, see ⑪②.

A 4WD hired from Tangalooma will need to be returned by 5pm. There is a 4pm launch back to the mainland, but a better option is to stay for dolphin-feeding *(see feature)* at sunset, and return to Brisbane on the 7pm launch.

Above from far left: feeding the dolphins; Tangalooma Wrecks; sand tobogganing.

Food and Drink

① BEACH CAFÉ
Tangalooma Island Resort; tel: 3410 6000; www.tangalooma.com; Mon–Fri 11.30am–2.30pm, Sat–Sun 11.30am–9pm; $$
This ultra-casual beachside café offers pizzas, pastas, burgers, salads and a delicious cold seafood platter, as well as children's meals.

② STEAKHOUSE
Tangalooma Island Resort; tel: 3410 6000; www.tangalooma.com; daily 6–9pm in season (check prior to visit); $$$
Any closer to the water and your feet would get wet at this laid-back alfresco restaurant, where succulent steaks and fresh seafood headline the menu, and a jacket and tie would look way out of place.

SUNSHINE COAST

Discover natural beauty and charming settlements by leaving the highway to pass through the eerie Glass House Mountains and remnant rainforests on the way to the ridge-top villages of Maleny and Montville, before descending to the chic beachside resort of Noosa.

The Croc Hunter
Australia Zoo started out as a small reptile park in the 1970s created by Bob and Lyn Irwin, but thanks to the antics with dangerous critters, most notably crocodiles, by their son, Steve 'The Crocodile Hunter' Irwin, it grew into a world-renowned zoo. Steve was tragically killed by a stingray in 2006, but his legacy of 'hands-on' conservation continues at the zoo.

DISTANCE 170km (106 miles)
TIME A full day
START Brisbane
END Noosa National Park
POINTS TO NOTE
You will need a car for this full-day tour *(see p.108)*; if you start by 8am, you can fit it all in with plenty of stops, but there's so much to see and so much worth doing on the Sunshine Coast that, if time permits, consider changing gears and stretching this tour into a two- or even three-day excursion. And if you time it to pass through Eumundi on a Wednesday or Saturday, try to catch the popular Eumundi Markets.

Food and Drink

① MARY CAIRNCROSS SCENIC RESERVE CAFÉ
148 Mountain View Road, Maleny; tel: 5494 2287; www.mary-cairncross.com.au; daily 8.30–4.30pm; $
If you skipped breakfast, this is your chance to refuel on organic muesli or eggs and bacon (at least until 11.30am). Lunch consists of variations of BLTs, burgers and salads. The coffee is organic and fairtrade, as befits the natural setting and panoramic views.

The Sunshine Coast is a glorious stretch of coastline extending about 120km (75 miles) from Bribie Island in the south to Rainbow Beach, near Fraser Island, in the north. Compared to the Gold Coast, commercial development is more restrained; though there are still high-rise towers and shopping malls, you are never too far away from a peaceful expanse of golden beach. Noosa is the jewel in the coastal crown, an unlikely encapsulation of luxury, hedonism and natural beauty that rarely fails to charm. Back from the beach, the rolling green hills of the hinterland are peppered with quaint villages and mysterious volcanic mountains. The red-cedar loggers are long gone (as are the red cedars), replaced by craftspeople, alternative lifestylers and bakers and baristas servicing the tourism boom.

GLASS HOUSE MOUNTAINS

Head north from Brisbane on the Bruce Highway approximately 56km (35 miles) and turn left at The Glasshouse Mountains Tourist Drive, also known as the Steve Irwin Way since the death of 'The Crocodile Hunter'

(see margin, opposite). This is where you will catch your first good glimpses of the **Glass House Mountains** ❶. These unusual volcanic plugs are the remains of lava-belching volcanoes that issued from the earth some 20 million years ago. The craggy, eroded peaks in the National Park (see www.derm.qld.gov. au) offer impressive walking tracks to panoramic lookouts, while the well-drained slopes of rich volcanic soil around the mountains are ideal for growing pineapples, which are sold at roadside stalls, along with avocados, macadamia nuts and other produce.

AUSTRALIA ZOO

About 2km (1¼ miles) past Beerwah, signs direct you to **Australia Zoo** ❷ (Steve Irwin Way, Beerwah; tel: 5436 2000; www.australiazoo.com.au; daily 9am–5pm; charge). With natural Australian and recreated Asian habitats, there are numerous mammals, birds and reptiles on display, as well as daily shows. You could easily spend half a day or more here, so note that bus tours from Brisbane and the Sunshine Coast are also available.

At Landsborough turn left, up the hill, following the signs and the winding road towards Maleny. As you climb, splendid views of patchwork farms and the coastline far to the east are revealed. There are many designated spots to stop the car, whip out the camera and admire the country.

MARY CAIRNCROSS SCENIC RESERVE

After 9km (5½ miles), turn left at Cairncross Corner off the main Maleny road, to **Mary Cairncross Scenic Reserve** ❸ (www.mary-cairncross. com.au; tel: 5429 6122). The reserve protects a remnant of the magnificent subtropical rainforest that once covered these ranges. There are easy trails, including ones that are wheelchair-accessible, through the rainforest and unobstructed views of the cultivated valleys, rugged Glass House Mountains and distant coastline. And if you are after a late breakfast or early lunch, head to the delightful **café**, see ⑪①.

Above from far left: Noosa; the Glass House Mountains.

Below: resident of Australia Zoo.

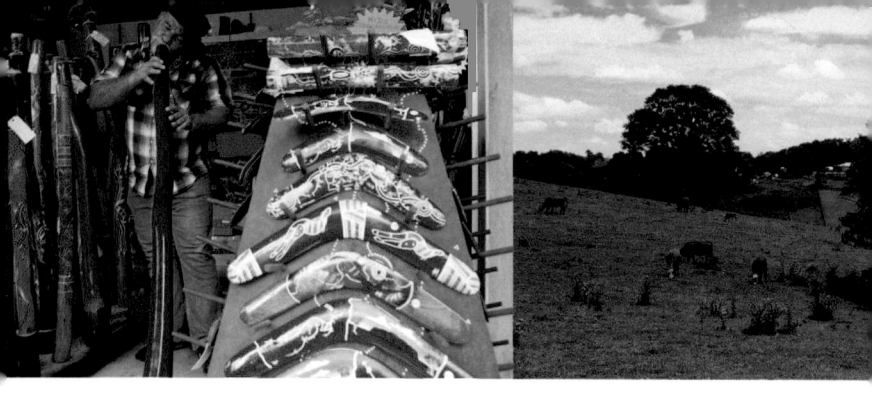

Eumundi Markets
The Eumundi Markets (Memorial Drive, Eumundi; Wed 8am–1.30pm and Sat 6.30am–2pm) started in 1979 as a few food stalls; today they are a 'must-do' for locals and visitors alike. Some 20,000 people descend to peruse hundreds of stalls selling local produce, arts and crafts, crystals and, well, just about everything.

MALENY

Continue on the same road for 9km (5½ miles), following the signposted tourist drive, which loops north to the hill township of **Maleny ❹**. Maleny is a picturesque country town of quaint colonial architecture occupied by new-age shops, galleries and craft outlets. Many talented artists and craftspeople have made this their home, and you may just find that something special here that is genuinely Australian and original.

MONTVILLE

Head east on the Maleny–Landsborough Road for 4km (2½ miles) before taking a left turn to **Montville ❺**, around 10km (6 miles) further north. Again you will enjoy spectacular ridge-top vistas, plus a few glimpses of scenic Lake Baroon. Montville, which visually is even more of a chocolate-box town than Maleny, is ornamented with determinedly quaint shops offering all manner of arts and crafts. The main street is well worth a wander, with numerous options for eating and drinking, such as **The Edge Restaurant**, see ⑪②.

EUMUNDI

Head east 15km (9 miles) to the Bruce Highway, then turn left towards Nambour to reach **Eumundi ❻** after 26km (16 miles). Another charming hinterland town, Eumundi is decorated with contemporary artwork and sculptures by local artists, and mingling with the historic buildings are shops selling new-age paraphernalia and jewellery, along with plenty of cafés. But it is the renowned markets *(see margin, left)* that have put Eumundi on the map. From Eumundi, it is 21km (13 miles) east via Route 12 to the coast at Noosa.

NOOSA

What is Noosa? The area includes Noosaville, set back on the Noosa River; Noosa Junction; and Sunshine Beach, but for most people the name means the compact area called **Noosa Heads ❼**.

Food and Drink

② THE EDGE RESTAURANT
The Mayfield Centre, 127–133 Main Street, Montville; tel: 5442 9344; 9am–4pm; $$
If you can take your eyes off the spectacular hinterland views that stretch away to the Pacific Ocean, you will find a light and seasonal Modern Australian menu of pasta dishes, salads, steaks and seafood such as salt-and-pepper prawns.

③ BISTRO C
49 Hastings Street, Noosa Heads; tel: 5447 2855; www.bistroc.com.au; daily 7.30am–10pm; $$$
This chic beachside restaurant epitomises the modern Australian dining scene, with an imaginative menu fusing the tastes of the Mediterranean and Asia with Australia's bounty of fresh ingredients. There are five separate, regularly changing menus throughout the day, with a wide-ranging selection from coconut chicken salad to caramelised pork belly.

Located on the sandy shore of Laguna Bay at the mouth of the river and overlooked by a ruggedly natural headland, its 'strip' is **Hastings Street,** where the chintziest shops, finest restaurants and beautiful people all come together epitomising the Noosa fairytale. Among the great choice of restaurants is the perfectly positioned **Bistro C**, see ⑪③, while all your information and booking needs are met by the **Noosa Visitor Centre** (Hastings Street; tel: 5430 5020; www. visitnoosa.com.au; daily 9am–5pm). Directly in front of Hastings Street is **Noosa Main Beach**, where you can learn to surf or just enjoy the golden sand and gentle waves.

Around Noosa Heads

Other places to explore locally include **Noosa National Park** ❼ on the headland east of town, and **Noosa North Shore**, across the river. The **Queensland Parks and Wildlife Service Information Centre** (daily 9am–3pm) in Noosa National Park is just minutes' walk from Hastings Street, and from there you can access trails where you might spot koalas and admire spectacular views of the Pacific Ocean and Sunshine Coast. Noosa North Shore is the start of the remote **Cooloola Coast**, which stretches up to **Rainbow Beach**. It is accessed by a ferry near Tewantin and is best explored by 4WD, but even without a 4WD, activities such as horse and camel

riding can be organised; ask at the Noosa Visitor Centre.

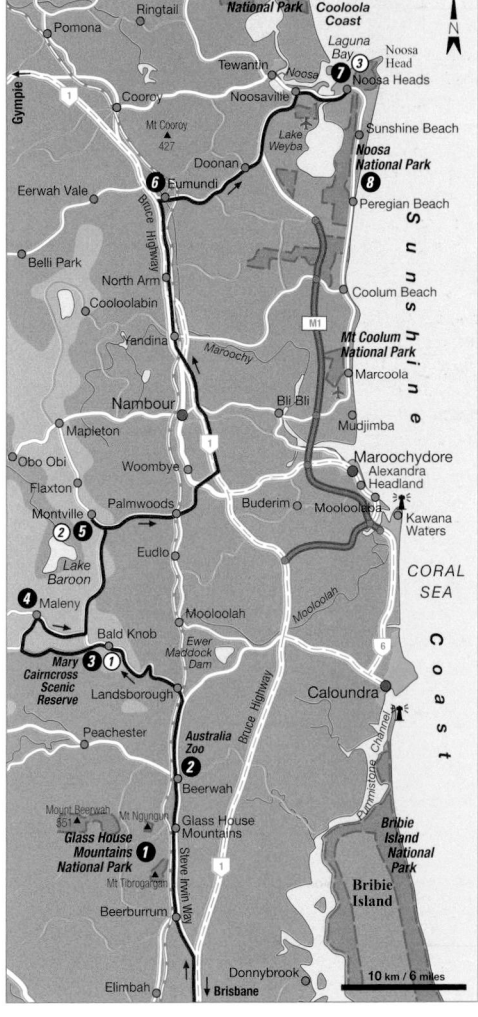

NORTH STRADBROKE ISLAND

North Stradbroke has long been Brisbane's favourite escape. Seemingly endless white-sand beaches, freshwater lagoons and wilderness walks will delight back-to-nature types. And for those who'd prefer not to go 'bush', there are also plenty of options for pampered relaxation and fine dining.

Jumpinpin

Jumpinpin is the name given to the tidal channel between North and South Stradbroke islands, dividing what was the singular Isle of Stradbroke. The story goes that islanders salvaged, among other things, a good deal of explosives from the wreck of the *Cambus Wallace* in 1894, which they detonated on the beach. A subsequent cyclone in 1896 provided sufficient winds and seas to erode the now weakened dunes and create the constantly shifting channel we see today.

DISTANCE 71km (44 miles), not including drive on Main Beach
TIME A full day
START/END Dunwich
POINTS TO NOTE
A 4WD is needed, although a conventional car is fine if you leave out the beach driving. Vehicle ferries and water taxis access the island from Cleveland Ferry Terminal, 35km (22 miles) southeast of Brisbane CBD; to catch a 9am ferry, leave Brisbane by 7.45am. The ferry crossing takes 45 minutes.

Ferry operators include Sea Stradbroke Car & Passenger Ferry (tel: 3488 9777; www.seastradbroke.com) and Stradbroke Ferries (tel: 3488 5300; www.stradbrokeferries.com.au). You must book in advance, and the ferry company can arrange your beach access (driving) permit. Along with the permit, you will get a tide chart as beach driving is prohibited an hour either side of high tide.

North Stradbroke, 'Straddie' to the locals, is an island of immense natural beauty, and at 38km (24 miles) long and 11km (7 miles) wide, it is the world's second-largest sand island. It has been home to the Nunukul, Nughie and Goenpul tribes, who know it as Minjerribah, for thousands of years. Indeed, artefacts of Aboriginal settlement date back over 20,000 years. European settlement dates back around 185 years with the establishment of a shipping pilot station at Amity Point. The island was (re)named in honour of the son of the first Earl of Stradbroke, H.J. Rous, the captain of the ship conveying Governor Darling on his first inspection of the Moreton Bay penal settlement in 1827. Today's small permanent population of approximately 3,000 swells considerably at weekends and during holidays.

DUNWICH

The small fishing township of **Dunwich ❶**, lapped by the calm waters of Moreton Bay, has a fascinating and

varied history. The Europeans used Dunwich as a convict outstation, a Catholic mission, a quarantine station and then a benevolent institution. A heritage walking trail connects many buildings remaining from this period and winds through convict relics and graves dating back to those shipwrecked in the 1800s. Pick up details from the **Stradbroke Island Tourist Information Centre** (Junner Street; tel: 3409 9555; www.stradbroke tourism.com; daily 8.30am–4.30pm).

The **North Stradbroke Island Historical Museum** (15–17 Welsby Street; tel: 3409 9699; www.stradbroke museum.com; Tue–Sat 10am–2pm; charge), housed in an original dormitory of the benevolent institution, offers an impressive display of photographs and items retrieved from shipwrecks, as well as information about Aboriginal and pioneer settlements and the sand-mining industry.

POINT LOOKOUT

From Dunwich, drive 19km (12 miles) northeast to the township of **Point Lookout ②**. Point Lookout is Queensland's most easterly point, named by James Cook in 1770. The

Above from far left: Brown Lake; aerial view of Dunwich.

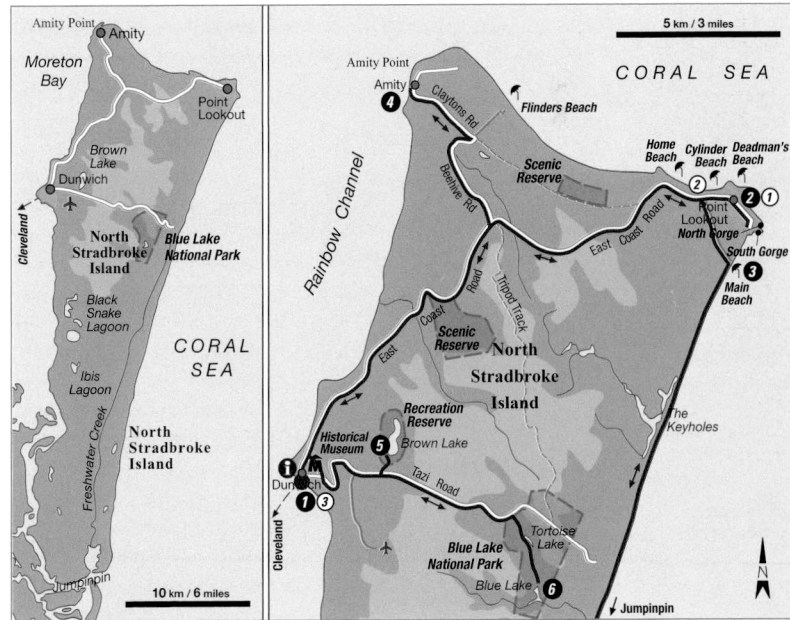

Whale-Watching

Point Lookout is one of the best land-based vantage points to witness the acrobatic antics of magnificent humpback whales. Flipper-slapping, tail-waving and mighty breaching leaps that result in explosive splashdowns can all be witnessed as the whales pass by from June to November on their annual migration north. All summer they have been feeding in the rich waters of Antarctica and now they are heading for their calving grounds in the Coral Sea.

Below: heading to Home Beach.

rocky headland shelters several excellent beaches, such as Deadman's (unpatrolled but good for exploring rock pools), Cylinder (patrolled surf beach and ideal for families), Home (unpatrolled) and Flinders (unpatrolled and 4WD allowed).

Do what Cook certainly did not do and grab a refreshing morning tea break at the **Oceanic Gelati & Coffee Bar**, see ⑪①, and then cross the road to start the spectacular **North Gorge Walk** (the path begins beside the public toilet block). It's only a little over 1km (⅔ mile) and the views are superb. As the pathway clings to the edge of the coast, watch out for humpback whales *(see margin, left)*. There are often large pods of dolphins, graceful manta rays, sharks and turtles, all swimming freely in the sparkling blue waters below. In places

you can walk out onto the rocky coastline to sit and watch the wildlife show and the powerful waves crashing ashore. Further along, the walk ventures onto **South Gorge** and then the sweeping expanse of Main Beach comes into view. As the path ends and heads towards the road, turn right and you will find you are only a short distance away from your starting point.

The views from Point Lookout are truly sublime, and to continue the experience over lunch, drive back along the road you came in on to the **Stradbroke Island Beach Hotel & Spa Resort**, see ⑪②, known to locals as the Straddie Pub. In whale-watching season you can sit and eat your fresh fish and chips while watching whales breach and splash below.

MAIN BEACH

Just to the west of the Straddie Pub there is a turnoff to the south onto George Nothling Drive, with signposts indicating access to **Main Beach** ❸. Before heading down there, consult your tide chart as beach driving is best an hour or so either side of low tide and prohibited an hour either side of high tide. This amazing stretch of pristine white beach is legendary with Stradbroke regulars. Surfers rise to the challenge on these waves, fishermen cast into the deep 'gutters' (channels between the breaks), pulling in dinner, and you can easily find a patch of

Above from far left: enjoying the view on the North Gorge Walk; Main Beach; Amity Jetty.

lonely beach to comb. Or just revel in the fact that you can drive along the sand with the wind in your hair. It is possible to drive the entire 34km (21-mile) length to **Jumpinpin**, the point where North and South Stradbroke islands were once connected *(see margin, p.52)*.

AMITY POINT

It is a 12km (7½ mile) drive west from Point Lookout to **Amity ④** for a look at this down-to-earth fishing village on the island's northwestern tip. Families come here for the beachside camping, calm waters and safe swimming, and a place to dangle a fishing line. A pilot station was established here in 1825; hence Amity became the main access point for boats coming from Brisbane over the next 150 years.

BROWN AND BLUE LAKES

From Amity Point, retrace your drive back out onto the East Coast Road and turn right for Dunwich. If you have time to spare before your return ferry, **Brown Lake ⑤** is only 4km (2½ miles) east of Dunwich, and it is worth taking a glimpse at this perched lake, part of the island's unique freshwater lake system. The tea-brown colour comes from the surrounding trees, reeds and organic matter; nevertheless, you can take a refreshing swim or wander the walking trail around its shore. Alternatively, **Blue Lake ⑥** is 10km (6 miles) east of Dunwich (accessible by a conventional car), and from the carpark it is a further 3km (1¾-mile) walk (approximately 30 minutes). The gin-like waters lap clean white sand and become deep blue as the waters deepen. Wildlife, such as swamp wallabies and sand goannas, abounds, especially in the early morning or late afternoon.

Head back to Dunwich to catch the ferry back to Brisbane, and if there is time for an afternoon tea stop, visit the **Island Fruit Barn**, see ⑪③, in town.

Food and Drink

① OCEANIC GELATI & COFFEE BAR
19 Mooloomba Road, Point Lookout; tel: 3415 3222; daily 9.30am–5pm; $
Choose from a great range of fruit juices, smoothies, gelati and coffee. Especially good is the affogato, espresso poured over ice cream.

② STRADBROKE ISLAND BEACH HOTEL & SPA RESORT
East Coast Road, Point Lookout; tel: 3409 8188; www.stradbrokehotel.com.au; daily 7.30–10am, 11.30am–2.30pm, 5.30–8.30pm; $$$
Overlooking the beach, the bistro and beer garden of the 'Straddie Pub' offer an excellent choice of local seafood, including Straddie prawns and beer-battered coral trout, plus succulent steaks, pizzas, and meals for 'nippers'.

③ ISLAND FRUIT BARN
16 Bingle Road, Dunwich; tel: 3409 9125; Mon–Fri 7am–5pm, Sat–Sun 7am–4pm; $$
This atypical fruit barn adds value to its array of seasonal fruits and vegetables by tempting travellers with fresh salads, organic fruit smoothies, delicious cakes and decent coffee.

GOLD COAST

Queensland's Gold Coast is not just a surfer's paradise. On this driving tour you can certainly catch its waves, but also explore its golden shores and glittering malls, take to its high-rise towers, and discover its quiet corners and natural charm.

DISTANCE 102km (63 miles)
TIME A full day
START Brisbane
END Currumbin Wildlife Sanctuary
POINTS TO NOTE

Don't forget your swimming gear, hat and sunscreen. If time permits, extend your stay to enjoy fully the theme parks *(see p.24)*, surf and plethora of natural and man-made attractions; you can also combine this tour with tour 7 *(p.60)*. For accommodation suggestions *see p.113–14*.

The Gold Coast is easily accessed by bus or train-and-bus combination from Brisbane, and there are bus connections directly from Brisbane Airport. The Gold Coast also has its own airport at Coolangatta, 25km (15½ miles) south of Surfers Paradise.

Food and Drink

① **MAX BRENNER CHOCOLATE BAR**
Ground Floor, Marina Mirage, 74 Seaworld Drive, Main Beach; tel: 5591 1588; www.maxbrenner. com.au; Mon–Thur 10am–10pm, Fri 10am–midnight, Sat 9am–midnight, Sun 9am–10pm; $$
If you can't resist the smells wafting from the doorway, sit down surrounded by everything chocolate to drink or munch on. Coffee is also available.

The post-war boom of the 1940s saw this area wake to a future of opportunity, and the opportunists have continued to make it their home. The hedonistic lifestyle and garishness that characterises the high-rise section of The Strip culminates in Surfers Paradise, Queensland's answer to Miami or Ipanema. However, the Gold Coast is not only a stretch of golden beaches with a backdrop of skyscrapers, a concentration of colourful theme parks and conspicuous commercialism. As you move along the coast away from 'Paradise', you can find a more natural beauty. The surf beaches, particularly Burleigh Heads set in National Parkland, remain strikingly gorgeous.

MAIN BEACH

From Brisbane, drive southeast for 64km (40 miles) on the Southeast Freeway (Route 3), which becomes the Pacific Motorway (Route 1). You will pass signs to several theme parks *(see p.24)*, as most are concentrated at the northwestern end of the coastal strip, just off the motorway. At Helensvale, turn off at Exit 62 onto the Gold Coast Highway for 13km (8 miles) to **Main Beach ❶**. This has long been a favoured spot for the stylish and wealthy and those who enjoy chic boutiques and being seen in trendy cafés.

The Spit is a 3km (2-mile) sandbar running north of Main Beach, separating the Broadwater from the Pacific Ocean. Head along Seaworld Drive, where, on the left, you will find the **Marina Mirage** (www.marinamirage.com.au; daily 10am–6pm), a luxury boat marina combined with an upmarket shopping complex of fashion boutiques, cafés and restaurants. Indulge in chocolate for morning tea at **Max Brenner Chocolate Bar**, see ⑪①, drop in to admire the opulence of the **Palazzo Versace Hotel** next door, or window-shop the classy boutiques.

Also adjacent to Marina Mirage is **Mariners Cove (Fisherman's Wharf)**, with yet more dining options as well as numerous companies offering watersport activities from fishing to jet boating. Further along the Spit is **Sea World** *(see p.24)*.

SURFERS PARADISE

Continue south on the Gold Coast Highway for 3km (2 miles) to **Surfers Paradise ❷**, the flashy pendant on this stretch of coastline bling. It was the surf that first lured people to these beaches, and it's the surf that is still the prime attraction, so factor in some time

Above from far left: viewing floor on QDeck; Main Beach.

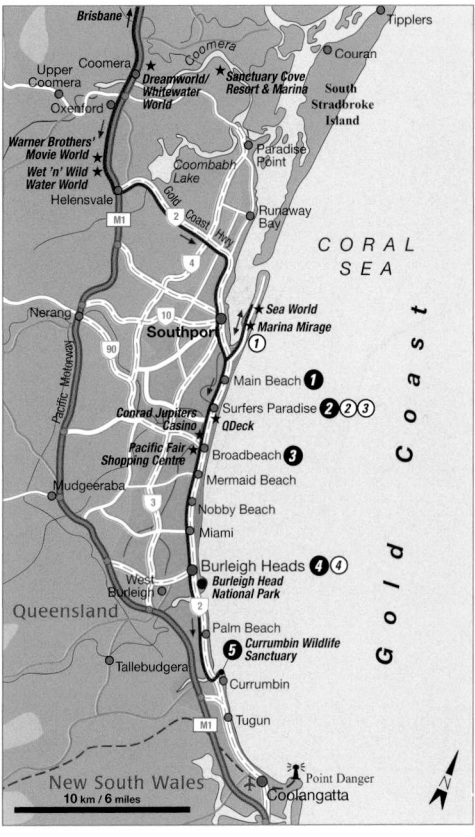

Meter Maids

Meter Maids were introduced to Surfers Paradise in 1965 to put a positive spin on the fact that parking meters were installed on the tourist strip. Clad in tiaras and gold bikinis, pretty girls walked the streets putting coins into meters. They attracted worldwide attention and, despite the controversial and anachronistic portrayal of women, have been part of the Gold Coast landscape ever since.

to enjoy it. Why not take in a surfboard-riding lesson *(see feature)*, or just take some beach time after the drive.

When you're done with swimming, surfing or just lying about, check out **QDeck** (Q1 Surfers Paradise Boulevard; tel: 5582 2700; www.qdeck.com. au, Sun–Thur 9am–9pm, Fri–Sat 9am–midnight; charge), one of the Gold Coast's essential attractions. Here you will ascend to Level 77 of the world's tallest residential building, rising 322m (1,056ft) into the sky for breathtaking 360-degree views that extend up and down the coast from Brisbane to Byron Bay.

For lunch beside the ocean with a dose of Aussie beach culture, walk a few blocks south along the shoreline to the **Northcliffe Surf Lifesaving**

Club, see ⑪②. Or, if you're returning through Surfers in the evening, head to the shopping and apartment complex, Circle on Cavill, for **Perle Contemporary Dining and Lounge Bar**, see ⑪③.

BROADBEACH

A short 2km (1¼ miles) south is **Broadbeach ❸**, a slightly less frenetic and more family-friendly town than Surfers, but still a zone of residential towers, shopping malls and tempting eateries. If you haven't had enough retail therapy, turn right into Hooker Boulevard and stop at **Pacific Fair Shopping Centre** (www.pacificfair. com.au; Fri–Wed 9am–5.30pm, Thur 9am–9pm), one of the largest shopping malls in the Southern Hemisphere and jam-packed with fashion stores. Across the road, just a few minutes' walk away, is **Conrad Jupiters Casino** (www.jupiterscasino.com.au; daily 24 hours). With seven restaurants and five bars, plus the gaming tables and machines, there's seemingly no end to the ways you can lighten your wallet here.

BURLEIGH HEADS

A further 8km (5 miles) south brings you to **Burleigh Heads ❹**, the Gold Coast's premier family destination. Here the beaches are backed by beautiful parkland, and you can sit on the grass under beachside pines and palms

Learn to Surf

The Gold Coast is one of the great surfing meccas of the world, with excellent beach breaks all along the coast, so it makes sense to grab both a board and an instructor to give the sport a try. Beginner lessons are generally two hours long, and start with honing your technique on the sand before heading to the water for the exhilaration of standing up on your board for the first time. Several surf schools are located up and down the coast. At the Cheyne Horan School of Surf (The Esplanade, Surfers Paradise; tel:1800 227 873; www.cheynehoran.com.au), the former world surfing champion and his small team of instructors offer daily beginner classes at 10am and 2pm, as well as complimentary hotel pick-up anywhere from Broadbeach to Southport.

while watching the surfers take on some of Australia's best waves. For beachside dining you would be hard-pressed to beat **Mermaids Café & Bar**, see ⑪④.

Burleigh Head National Park (veer left along Goodwin Terrace as you come into Burleigh Heads) is also great for views. If you have a spare hour and are keen to stretch your legs, the 2.5km (1½-mile) **Ocean View Circuit** leads around the rocky headland from Tallebudgera Creek to the southern edge of Burleigh Heads Township.

CURRUMBIN WILDLIFE SANCTUARY

Six kilometres (4 miles) south of Burleigh Heads is one of the Gold Coast's oldest tourist attractions, **Currumbin Wildlife Sanctuary** ❺ (28 Tomewin Street, Currumbin; tel: 1300 886 531; www.cws.org.au; daily 8am–5pm; charge). The sanctuary continues to delight kids of all ages with interactive wildlife displays. In addition to the various shows during the day, the **Wildnight Adventure** starts with a buffet dinner (5.30–7pm) before a nocturnal guided tour.

From Currumbin you can head back to Brisbane, about 100km (63 miles) away on the Pacific Motorway, or find accommodation on the Gold Coast *(see p.113)* and continue the tour of the Gold Coast Hinterland *(see p.60)*.

Food and Drink

② NORTHCLIFFE SURF LIFESAVING CLUB BISTRO
At Garfield Terrace and Thornton Street, Surfers Paradise; tel: 5539 8091; www.northcliffesurfclub. com.au; daily 7.30am–9pm; $$
Beachside surf lifesaving clubs are iconically Australian, and at this one you can watch the action on the beach while enjoying a casual and extensive menu that includes everything from burgers, baguettes, sandwiches, pasta and pizza to chargrilled meats and seafood dishes.

③ PERLE CONTEMPORARY DINING AND LOUNGE BAR
Circle on Cavill, 3184 Surfers Paradise Boulevard; www.perle dining.com; tel: 5538 2141; daily 6am–9.30pm; $$$
For some culinary pampering, this venue boasts a lavish decor, floor-to-ceiling wine cellar and creative menu of modern Australian cuisine. Try the fillet of snapper poached in a Thai lemongrass and kaffir lime leaf coconut cream broth, served with a *pad thai*-inspired salad.

④ MERMAIDS CAFÉ & BAR
43 Goodwin Tce, Burleigh Heads; tel: 5520 1177; www.mermaidson burleigh.com; daily 7.30am–9.30pm; $$$
Sit on the balcony that spills out onto the beach and enjoy the 'Mediterasian' menu, including steaks, seafood chowder with seared scallops, or Balmain bugs with wakame and green pawpaw, all accompanied by great wines and coffee.

Above from far left: dusk view of the Gold Coast; feeding time at Currumbin Wildlife Sanctuary.

Schoolies
The very mention of the word can bring a shudder to parents of teenagers. Somehow, post-exam celebrations for final-year students has become a ritual, and Surfers Paradise the pilgrimage of choice for 'schoolies' from all over Australia. Come the end of November they descend en masse – a cocktail of youthful exuberance, concerts, alcohol and chemicals that can continue until the middle of December. You have been warned.

GOLD COAST HINTERLAND

Behind the cement-and-glass forests of the Gold Coast is a verdant hinterland of rugged ranges sheltering villages, plunging waterfalls and nature retreats. Much of this stunning landscape is protected in three National Parks: Tamborine, Lamington and Springbrook.

> **DISTANCE** 170km (105 miles)
> **TIME** Two days
> **START** Oxenford turnoff
> **END** Springbrook National Park
> **POINTS TO NOTE**
> This is a driving tour. From Brisbane head southeast for about 60km (37 miles) on the Southeast Freeway (Route 3), which becomes the Pacific Motorway (Route 1), exiting at Oxenford. If you are starting this tour from the Gold Coast, either head north along the Gold Coast Highway and the Pacific Motorway to exit at Oxenford, or access the Pacific Motorway at Nerang. From Oxenford, take the Mount Tamborine Road west and follow it for about 2km (1¼ miles) before turning right on a 19km (12-mile) route that takes you to Eagle Heights.

Tamborine Mountain Distillery
Australia's smallest operating pot distillery, Tamborine Mountain (87–91 Beacon Road, North Tamborine; tel: 5545 3452; www.tamborine mountaindistillery. com; Mon–Sat 10am–3pm) has won international awards for its liqueurs, schnapps, vodkas and fruit brandies, which are flavoured by the amazing range and quality of fruit grown on Mount Tamborine's rich volcanic soils. The delightful organic farm and distillery with cellar-door sales is well worth a detour.

and glorious natural vistas. The bush that forms the Gold Coast's green backdrop is in stark contrast to the hype of the coastal strip and is the ideal hangover cure for the party lifestyle. The rugged ranges that challenged the pioneers and cedar-getters now embrace well-being spas, wineries, cheese factories and craft stalls. There are also several 'islands' of native bush protected in National Parks offering idyllic nature-focused retreats.

MOUNT TAMBORINE

The winding road from the **Oxenford turnoff** on the Pacific Motorway ascends for 19km (12 miles) through a mixture of native bush and rolling pastures to Eagle Heights with sweeping views of the Gold Coast, its hinterland and the ocean beyond. This mountain oasis comprises the three close-knit heritage communities of Mount Tamborine, North Tamborine and Eagle Heights, and is collectively referred to as **Mount Tamborine**. The **Visitor Information Centre** (Doughty

About an hour's drive from either Brisbane or the Gold Coast high-rises is this realm of lush rainforests, waterfalls

Park, Main Western Road, North Tamborine; tel: 5545 3200; www. tamborinemtncc.org.au; daily 10am–3.30pm) can provide maps of the local roads, bushwalks and National Parks.

Eagle Heights

Gallery Walk in **Eagle Heights ❶** is the mountain community's shopping precinct and is filled with an array of touristy craft shops, galleries and alfresco eateries. For morning tea head to **Granny Macs Store**, see ⑪①. Continue to the end of Gallery Walk (it turns into Long Road) and turn left into Curtis Road. At the end of this road there is access to a beautiful 900m/yd rainforest walk to **Cedar Creek Falls**, part of **Tamborine National Park ❷**. If you are extending your stay there are many other great walks in this National Park that comprises 14 separate parcels of land, one of which, **Witches Falls**, was Queensland's first National Park. **St Bernards Hotel**, see ⑪②, at Mount Tamborine makes a good stop for lunch or refreshments.

LAMINGTON NATIONAL PARK

From North Tamborine take the Tamborine Mountain Road south to Mount Tamborine and continue towards Canungra, turning left at the Canungra–Nerang crossroads and right a little further on at the Beechmont/Binna Burra road. You have

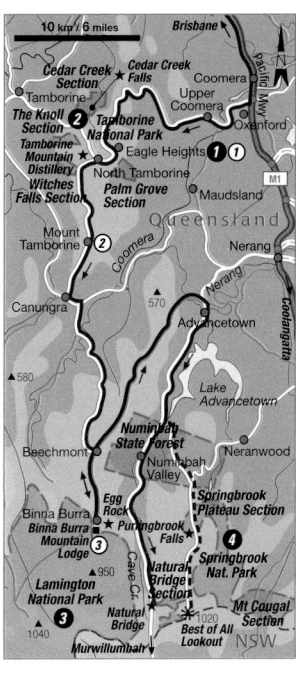

Above: view from Mount Tamborine.

Food and Drink

① **GRANNY MACS STORE**
139 Gallery Walk, Eagle Heights; tel: 5545 1999; www. grannymacs.com.au; daily 9am–4.30pm; $
Relax on the veranda and enjoy Devonshire tea, pancakes, or a light meal such as soup or salad. The store is also renowned for its wide variety of fudge made on the premises.

② **ST BERNARDS HOTEL**
101 Alpine Terrace, Mount Tamborine; tel: 5545 1177; www.stbernardshotel.com; noon–2pm, 6–9pm; $$
Venerable St Bernards has the ambience of a country pub far removed from the chintzy fudge shops and galleries that dominate the mountain. Enjoy hearty pub food, such as salt-and-pepper calamari and eye fillet steak, served with just enough flair to keep it interesting.

Above from far left:
Cave Creek; King-
fisher Bay Resort.

Purlingbrook Falls
The Springbrook
Plateau section of the
National Park is rich in
natural beauty, excel-
lent bushwalks and
stunning waterfalls.
Highly recommended
is the 4km (2½-mile)
Purlingbrook Falls
circuit walk (allow 2–3
hours) that starts from
the Gwongorella
picnic area. To get
there, return down the
Nerang–Murwillumbah
road and, after 11km
(7 miles), turn right
and right again onto
the Springbrook Road
(Route 99). The
Dancing Waters Cafe
next to the car park is
a good bet for a
snack or a light lunch.
Additionally, the Best
of All Lookout lives up
to its name.

now descended into the **Coomera River Valley** and are climbing the opposite ridge to the hilltop village of Beechmont. Turn right here for the 10km (6-mile) drive to **Binna Burra Mountain Lodge** *(see p. 114)*, 800m (2,600ft) above sea level, in the World Heritage-listed 20,000ha (50,000-acre) **Lamington National Park ❸**. The lodge was the first resort in the region to gain official ecotourism accreditation.

Detailed walking maps and park brochures are available at the **National Parks and Wildlife Information Centre** (tel: 5533 3584; Mon–Fri 7.30am–4pm, Sat and Sun 9am–3pm), just before the Lodge. The **Rainforest Circuit** is an easy 30-minute walk, while the short **Bellbird Lookout Walk** offers excellent views of towering rocky bluffs and the Numinbah Valley. The valley used to be the forest habitat of the valuable hoop pine and the red cedar, the harvesting of which led to the establishment of the first European settlement here, which in

turn ultimately resulted in the clearing of the valley. Sit down and enjoy the views over a coffee or lunch at the **Binna Burra Mountain Lodge**, see ⑪③; dinner could be taken in the lodge's Clifftop Dining Room.

SPRINGBROOK NATIONAL PARK

Return down the same route via Beech-mont, but turn right close to the bottom of the hill and take the Nerang–Murwillumbah road (Route 97) via Advancetown. This takes you up the scenic **Numinbah Valley** to the **Natural Bridge** (also known as the Natural Arch) section of **Springbrook National Park ❹**. About 25km (15 miles) from the Advancetown turn-off, you will find the Natural Bridge car park. A 1km (⅔-mile) circular walk brings you to this peculiar formation where **Cave Creek** stream plunges through the eroded roof of an underground basalt cavern. You can enter further down the pathway to view the waterfall. For more waterfalls, make the detour to take the **Purlingbrook Falls** circuit walk *(see margin, left)*.

From Natural Bridge it is 100km (62 miles) to Brisbane. Head back down the Nerang–Murwillumbah Road, continue straight on the Beaudesert–Nerang Road, following signs to Nerang. At Nerang you will merge onto the Pacific Motorway for the 71km (44-mile) trip back to Brisbane.

Food and Drink 🍴

③ BINNA BURRA MOUNTAIN LODGE
Binna Burra Mountain Lodge, Lamington National Park;
tel: 1300 246 622; www.binnaburralodge.com.au; Mon–Fri
9.30am–3pm, Sat–Sun 7.30am–4pm; $$
Enjoy the sweeping ridge-top views over the rainforest,
Numbah Valley and the coast, while choosing from a casual
lunch and tea menu, including burgers, salads and scones
in the Lamington Tea House. Hearty breakfasts and dinners
are served up in the Cliff Top Dining Room.

FRASER ISLAND

This three-day 4WD adventure takes you to an extraordinary wilderness where flourishing rainforests, pristine freshwater lakes and streams and desert-like sand dunes are accessed by long, lonely highways of sand. This is the world's largest sand island and an area of rare beauty.

Fraser Island was listed as a Unesco World Heritage Area in 1992, recognising its significant natural features, including dune, lake and forest ecosystems. A great variety of plant communities on the island grow entirely on sand and range from coastal heath to mangrove forests, swamps and subtropical rainforests.

Evidence suggests that the indigenous Butchulla people (now living on the mainland) occupied these parts for more than 5,500 years. Their name for the island was K'gari, which means paradise, and that it certainly is. Although logging, then sand mining become major industries after European discovery, they were halted a couple of decades ago, allowing Fraser island to recover its natural state.

KINGFISHER BAY RESORT

From River Heads, it takes 50 minutes to reach **Kingfisher Bay Resort ❶**. This, the larger of the island's two resorts, nestles on the edge of the Great Sandy Strait on Fraser Island's western shore. It is a multi-award-winning

DISTANCE 157km (97 miles) on day two drive

TIME Three days

START/END Kingfisher Bay

POINTS TO NOTE

For the 12.30pm ferry to the island from River Heads, 300km (186 miles) north of Brisbane, leave the city by 7am. Take the Bruce Highway to the Maryborough exit and follow signs to Hervey Bay and River Heads. Collect your pre-booked ticket (www.fraserisland ferry.com.au) at least 20 minutes prior to departure. You can also fly to Hervey Bay or take a long-distance bus *(see p.108)*. River Heads has a café and store to buy picnic supplies for lunch.

Hire a 4WD vehicle in Brisbane, Hervey Bay or at Kingfisher Bay Resort. A beach-driving permit must be obtained, either from Queensland Parks and Wildlife Service (tel: 131304; www.epa.qld. gov.au) or from the ferry before you board. For accommodation at Kingfisher Bay Resort, *see p.114*.

Guided Island Tours

If you are not confident to do this 4WD tour on your own, there are many tour operators offering guided tours from Brisbane and Hervey Bay, including Cool Dingo Tours (tel: 1800 072 555; www. cooldingotour.com), Sunrover Expeditions (tel: 3202 4241; www. sunrover.com.au) and Bushwacker Ecotours (tel: 1300 559 355; www. bushwacker-ecotours. com.au). Another option is to drive to Kingfisher Bay Resort and join one of the resort's ranger-guided day tours.

Above from left:
sand driving with a 4WD; Wanggoolba Creek; rusty remnants of the *Maheno*.

ecotourism resort with accommodation designed to conserve energy, minimise waste and blend with the surrounding bush. On arrival follow signs to the reception for check-in.

Beach Driving
When driving on the beach all standard road rules apply, including keeping to the left of oncoming vehicles *(see p.109)*. Small aircraft also use the Seventy-Five Mile Beach (Eastern Beach) as a landing strip. Aeroplanes need to land on the harder sand found close to the water's edge, so vehicles should move to the upper beach nearer the high tide line. The best beach driving will be at low tide or within two hours either side.

[Map of Fraser Island with labels: Sandy Cape, CORAL SEA, Rooney Point, Marloo Bay, Waddy Point, Champagne Pools, Orchid Beach, Indian Head 6, Platypus Bay, Great Sandy National Park, Seventy-Five Mile Beach, The Pinnacles, Fraser Island, Maheno 5, Eli Creek, Moon Pt, Sandy Pt, Lake Garawongera, Happy Valley, Big Woody Island, Rainbow Gorge, Hervey Bay, Cornwells Break Rd, Kingfisher Bay Resort 4 1, Lake McKenzie 2, River Heads, Central Station 3, Eurong 4 2 3, Lake Wabby 7, Brisbane, Susan, Lake Birrabeen, Lake Boomanjin, Ungowa, Dilli Village, Poona National Park, Great Sandy Strait, Tuan, Hook Point, 20 km / 12 miles]

LAKE MCKENZIE

On the first afternoon, take to the island's inland bush tracks, following signs from the resort, to drive 12km (7 miles) southeast to Lake McKenzie. From now on you will be driving on sand tracks, generally only wide enough for one vehicle, so it is important to be vigilant for oncoming 4WDs. The drive time will depend on the condition of the track: if conditions are dry and rough, vehicles may become bogged *(see p.109)* and cause delays to your journey. A good run from Kingfisher Bay to Lake McKenzie will take 45 minutes, but it could take double that. Remember to pack water and food, as there are no facilities en route.

At the end of your winding drive through lush vegetation, **Lake McKenzie ❷** will dazzle you with its translucent blue water washing above pure white sand. Sitting 100m (330ft) above sea level and covering more than 150ha (370 acres), this perched lake is not fed by streams or groundwater but contains only rainwater filtered by the sand, making the water so pure it can support very little life.

Take the time to swim and laze on the soft sandy shores, before returning to Kingfisher Resort for sunset cocktails out on the jetty, or a stroll along the beach before a buffet-style dinner where the focus is on locally sourced ingredients at **Maheno Restaurant**, see ⑪①.

CENTRAL STATION

The order in which you do things on the second day out will be determined by tide times. Time your beach travel to an hour before and after low tide. The following itinerary has been based on low tide in the middle of the day.

After breakfast, depart by 8am for the 14km (7-mile) drive southeast to Central Station. From the resort, take the first sign that says Lake McKenzie. At the next junction, take a right turn onto Bennett Road, follow for approximately 6km (4 miles), then turn left at the next junction.

Originally an old logging depot, **Central Station 3** crouches under towering bunya pines and is now the starting point for many pretty walks into the surrounding areas. The **Pile Valley Circuit Walk** is a 4.5km (3-mile) boardwalk around **Wanggoolba Creek**, an astonishingly clear and pristine stream. The walk then winds through awesome satinay trees that grow to more than 60m (197ft).

Return to your vehicle and continue 8km (5 miles) east, following the signs to Eurong Beach Resort.

SEVENTY-FIVE MILE BEACH

The small village of **Eurong 4** has a resort and limited facilities, but you can buy petrol and a small selection of groceries. There is one café, the **Eurong Beach Resort Restaurant**, see 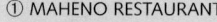②, and a **bakery**, see ③, which is a good place to buy a picnic lunch.

From Eurong Beach Resort, continue your journey out onto **Seventy-Five Mile Beach**, to head 30km (19 miles) north to Eli Creek. As the name suggests, **Seventy-Five Mile Beach** is a 120km (75-mile) stretch of uninterrupted sand highway, also known as the Eastern Beach, running up the eastern side of the island and flanked by sand dunes and rolling ocean. Be alert to ocean surges, soft sand, and freshwater springs that run out from the dunes to the ocean, sometimes causing small washouts.

Dingo Danger

Fraser Island's dingoes are among the purest in the world. As hunters and scavengers, they are wild and unpredictable and have been known to attack humans, so keep all food secure and do not leave rubbish or scraps lying around. If you feel threatened by a dingo, stand up at your full height, face the dingo, keep eye contact and back confidently away.

Food and Drink

① MAHENO RESTAURANT
Kingfisher Bay Resort, Fraser Island; tel: 4120 3333; www.kingfisherbay.com; daily 6.30am–10pm; $$–$$$
Maheno operates with a 'Paddock to Plate' approach, which means where possible the produce is sourced locally. Dinner is buffet-style, offering a selection of hot and cold dishes including local fish, king prawns and their renowned mornay of Hervey Bay scallops.

② EURONG BEACH RESORT RESTAURANT
Eurong Beach; tel: 1800 111 808; www.eurong.com; daily 6.30am–8pm; $$
This casual restaurant with attached bar serves a buffet lunch (11.30am–2pm) of soup, salad and hot dishes, and overlooks an inviting free-form swimming pool.

③ EURONG BEACH RESORT BAKERY
Eurong Beach; tel: 1800 111 808; daily 7.30am–5pm; $
Pop in for a tasty selection of baked goods such as pastries, rolls, pizza and cakes.

Millions of litres of fresh water pour out of **Eli Creek** ❺ every hour, and visitors love to swim and float down the clear-flowing stream. For an elevated view of the creek, walk the 400m/yd **Eli Creek Boardwalk**; it takes about 15 minutes.

Keep driving for 5km (3 miles) to reach the rusting relic of the *Maheno*, a trans-Tasman passenger liner that ran aground in a cyclone in 1935.

Indian Head

From the *Maheno*, continue 25km (16 miles) north along the beach to Indian Head. On the way look for the colourful sand cliffs lining the shore near the stretch called Cathedral Beach. One section, called **The Pinnacles**, has a stunning display of yellows, browns, reds and oranges, sculpted by nature. On arrival at **Indian Head** ❻, climb to the top of this headland and you might spot whales, sharks, rays, turtles and large schools of fish in the waters below.

From Indian Head it is a 3km (2-mile) drive north to the **Champagne Pools**, saltwater rock pools especially beautiful at low tide, while at high tide waves crash over the rocks creating 'champagne bubbles'.

RETURN TO KINGFISHER BAY RESORT

The return journey back down the beach to Eurong is 63km (39 miles), but look out for a more direct sand track approximately 6km (4 miles) before you get to Eurong. Known as Cornwells Break Road, you can follow it from Seventy-Five Mile Beach for 15km (9 miles) back to **Kingfisher Bay Resort**, and dinner in the signature **Seabelle Restaurant**, see ⑪④.

LAKE WABBY

Lake Wabby ❼ is another of the island's stunning lakes, perfect for a morning swim on your third day. Set out early from the resort and turn left onto the Cornwells Break Road. After 13km (8 miles), turn right for Lake Wabby (the drive takes at least an hour). Park the car and walk the 15-minute trail to the lake, where you will be met by a desert of shifting sands called the **Stonetool Sand Blow** and the deep, emerald waters of Lake Wabby.

Leave enough time for your return journey to Kingfisher Bay Resort, and catch the return 2pm ferry back to River Heads to make it back to Brisbane by early evening.

Food and Drink 🍴

④ SEABELLE RESTAURANT

Kingfisher Bay Resort, Fraser Island; tel: 4120 3333; www. kingfisherbay.com; daily 6.30–10pm; $$$

Describing itself as a bush-tucker dining experience, Seabelle Restaurant offers dishes that are inspired by ingredients traditionally used by indigenous people. Try the K'gari signature plate of chargrilled crocodile, kangaroo and emu with bunya nut pesto, bush tomato chutney, rosella and chilli plum jam, with a lemon myrtle panna cotta for dessert.

WHITSUNDAY ISLANDS

On this five-day camping and kayaking tour you have the opportunity to connect with the 'other' Whitsundays. Away from the tourist crowds and pampering resorts, you will be following Aboriginal migration routes, sleeping under the stars, exploring lonely beaches and paddling your own adventure.

The Whitsunday Islands form one of the world's most scenic adventure playgrounds. Hundreds of secluded bays, coves and deserted beaches are dotted throughout these calm waters of the Coral Sea, which are sheltered by the Great Barrier Reef. For thousands of years, the Ngaro Aboriginal people lived throughout this area, journeying between the islands in bark canoes and leaving behind rock art, fish traps, stone tools and middens. By following part of the Ngaro Sea Trail you will follow in their footsteps while experiencing the region's natural splendour.

This is not the usual way to experience the Whitsundays; you will not be visiting lavish resorts or cruising in luxury vessels. For this tour, you must be prepared to be self-sufficient, but your rewards will be lonely white-sand beaches, ancient rock art and uncrowded snorkelling and swimming.

AIRLIE BEACH

Airlie Beach ❶ is the hub of the Whitsunday coast and your base for exploring the islands. It is a tourist town through and through, with accommodation

DISTANCE Varies
TIME Five days
START/END Airlie Beach
POINTS TO NOTE

Tents and cooking utensils can be hired and drinking water and food bought at Airlie Beach. A reasonable level of fitness is required for this tour, along with sturdy footwear, hat, sunscreen and insect repellent. The ideal months for camping are from May to December. Contact Whitsunday Island Camping Connections (tel: 4946 6285; www.whitsundaycamping.com.au) for booking island transfers. Fares include hire of snorkelling equipment and drinking water for your stay. They also hire out camping equipment.

Book campsites and buy camping permits from Queensland Parks and Wildlife Service (tel: 131304; www.qld.gov.au/camping). For detailed maps and camping and safety information, see www.derm.qld.gov.au/parks/whitsunday-ngaro-sea-trail.

Getting There
Located 1,085km (674 miles) from Brisbane and 634km (394 miles) from Cairns, Airlie Beach is served by long-distance buses *(see p.108)* that ply the east coast. You can also fly in: Hamilton Island Airport has flights to/from both Cairns and Brisbane, and Proserpine Airport has flights to/from Brisbane.

Above: pristine waters around Hamilton Island.

options for all budgets *(see p.115)* and a vibrant dining scene. Numerous travel agencies, posing as information centres, will vie for your patronage with sailing, diving, cruising options and more.

You can stock up on camping provisions here, and for that last restaurant meal before camping, head to **Deja Vu**, see ⑪①.

Shute Harbour

Shute Harbour ❷ is 10km (6 miles) east of Airlie Beach and is the home port for many of the vessels that service the resorts and islands. Whitsunday Island Camping Connections' 10m (30ft) barge, *Scamper*, designed to run up the beach to drop off campers and their gear, operates from here. The office is beside the water at the end of Shute Harbour Drive. Departure times from Shute Harbour are determined by tides, and usually there is one departure per day.

SOUTH MOLLE ISLAND

It takes just 15 minutes to transfer to the campsite at **Sandy Bay** ❸, on the southwestern corner of **South Molle Island**. Picnic tables and toilet facilities are available here. Be sure to keep your food well sealed, as native animals such as goannas, birds and possums are part of the experience, and they like to help themselves.

With 420ha (1,000 acres) of National Park, the island offers superb

Whitsunday Activities

In Airlie Beach there are many companies running day trips that include an island visit, coral snorkelling, and a swim at Whitehaven Beach. The Whitsundays are also a great place to learn to sail, charter or skipper your own boat *(see p.23)*. Scuba-diving is popular *(see p.27)*, with pristine coral reefs teeming with colourful marine life. Check out www.tourismwhitsundays.com.au for a taste of what is on offer.

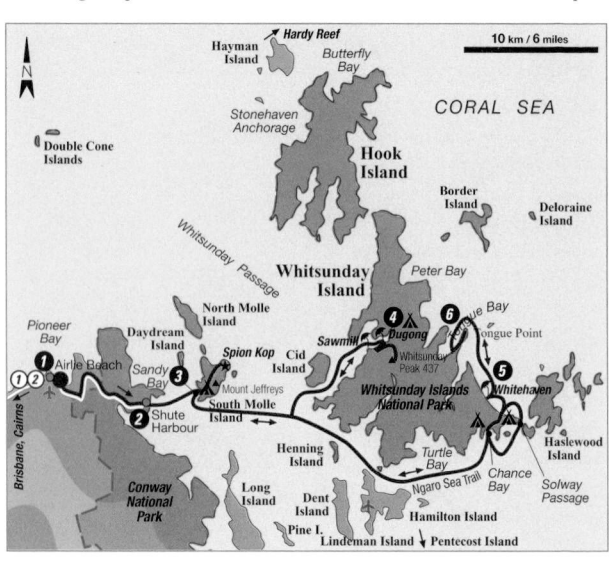

bushwalking. The walking tracks from Sandy Bay campsite to **Mount Jeffreys** and **Spion Kop** may be moderately challenging because of their length (the 11km (7-mile) return trip takes five hours); however, you are rewarded with spectacular views. South Molle has a diverse history of indigenous occupation, European settlement, grazing and tourism. The walk to Spion Kop passes a Ngaro quarry where the hillside is scattered with broken pieces of rock that were used to sharpen stone tools. Stone axes and other cutting tools have been found here.

WHITSUNDAY ISLAND

The *Scamper* will return for you the next day (transfer time is dependent on tides) for the 35-minute transfer to **Dugong Beach ❹**, your first camp on **Whitsunday Island**. From the beach, take the walking track to **Sawmill Beach** that leads on to **Whitsunday Peak**. This track may be one of the most challenging on the tour, reaching an elevation of 437m (1,400ft). It is a 5km (3-mile) return hike, and you should allow four hours to enjoy the views over the islands, turquoise waters and mainland. Steep, rocky hillsides support vine forest and open eucalypt forests, changing to grassland as you ascend. The unusual grass trees were once a source of food and tool material to the Ngaro,

Food and Drink
① DEJA VU
Golden Orchid Drive, Airlie Beach; tel: 4948 4309; www.airliebeach hotel.com.au; Wed–Sat noon–2.30pm, 6–9pm; $$$
This intimate poolside restaurant blends Indian, Mediterranean and Asian influences with fine Queensland produce. Whole Thai reef fish, signature goat curry and lamb rack with dolmades are just a small selection from the creative menu.

Whitsunday Resorts

Camping is not for everyone, and although just a handful of the 74 Whitsunday Islands are home to holiday resorts, these islands are the focus of most of the Whitsunday hype. Resorts range from the super-luxurious Hayman Island (www.hayman.com.au) to the backpacker-basic Hook Island Wilderness Resort (www.hookislandresort. com). Somewhere between these extremes lie the intimate eco-based luxury of Paradise Bay (www.paradisebay. com.au) on Long Island, the modest South Molle Island Resort (www.southmolleisland.com.au), the family-friendly resorts of Daydream Island (www.daydreamisland.com) and Lindeman Island (www.clubmed.com), and the large and popular Hamilton Island (www.hamiltonisland.com. au). Many of these resorts can be visited as a day guest from Airlie Beach or Shute Harbour, with connections operated by Cruise Whitsundays (tel: 4946 4662; www. cruisewhitsundays.com) or Fantasea Adventure Cruising (tel: 4967 5455; www.fantasea.com.au). And as a day guest you can still get to participate in resort activities, including watersports.

Above from left:
many of the ferry
services to the islands
leave from Shute Har-
bour; strolling along
the Cairns shore.

producing glue, fire sticks and spear handles and yielding starch, nectar and grubs. If you are lucky you will spot white-bellied sea eagles and brahminy kites soaring overhead. From May to September watch for the blows and splashes of humpback whales that use these warm waters as a calving ground.

Whitehaven Beach

Be ready for your 45-minute *Scamper* transfer to **Whitehaven Beach ❺** on the opposite side of Whitsunday Island. Ask Whitsunday Island Camping Connections to drop off kayaks (charge) for you to explore the coastline further. Brilliant white silica sand stretching for over 7km (4 miles) greets you on picture-postcard-perfect Whitehaven Beach. The beauty of camping overnight here is that you get to experience this paradise without the crowds. While the day-trippers are

basking on the sand, take the opportunity to follow the **Solway Circuit**, a 40-minute return walk, or continue on the **Chance Bay** walk, which is 7km (4 miles) long (there and back) and takes around four hours. Along this walk you will pass through beach scrub and grass-tree groves to cool cedar forests, and be rewarded with stunning views over Solway Passage to Haslewood Island and south to Pentecost and Hamilton islands.

Kayak to Tongue Bay

On the afternoon of the fourth day, take to the water in your kayak and listen for the exhalations of turtles (six of the world's seven marine species are found in the Whitsundays' waters) as you paddle 6km (4 miles) north to **Tongue Bay ❻**. Here you can tackle the **Tongue Point** walk, 3km (2 miles) and taking two hours return, to **Hill Inlet lookout**, with breathtaking views of Whitehaven Beach. As you paddle back to Whitehaven Beach camp, explore the rich mangrove forests that flourish along the shoreline.

Extend the Kayaking
If you enjoy being out
on the water, this trip
can be extended for
another two nights by
paddling north to
further sites on
Whitsunday Island
and to nearby Hook
Island. See www.
derm.qld.gov.au/
parks/whitsunday-
ngaro-sea-trail for
more details.

Food and Drink 🍴

② CAPERS AT THE BEACH
Airlie Beach Hotel, The Esplanade, Airlie Beach; tel: 4964 1777; www. airliebeachhotel.com.au; daily 7am–11am, noon–2.30pm, 6–9.30pm; $$$
Capers is a lively beachside restaurant offering a modern Australian menu of local seafood and sumptuous steaks. Their 'Localvore' menu uses ingredients sourced solely within 100km (60 miles) of the restaurant.

RETURN TO AIRLIE BEACH

On the morning of the fifth day, be ready for the one-hour *Scamper* transfer back to Shute Harbour and then reward your Robinson Crusoe efforts with dinner at **Capers at the Beach**, see ⑪②, in Airlie Beach.

CAIRNS

Cairns is a tropical outpost surrounded by a myriad natural charms and with more than a hint of colonial charisma. Set off on this leisurely stroll to capture some of the South Pacific magic that is too easily missed by the rush to head straight to the reef.

Cairns preserves much of its early beginnings as a port for inland gold-fields and as a centre for sugar-cane production, with several examples of tropical colonial architecture. Other industries have succeeded here, but none more so than the coral reef tourism that powers the town today.

MARLIN MARINA

Start at **Marlin Marina** ❶, the berth for the massive wave-piercing catama-rans that whisk people to the coral reefs day in day out. At the **Reef Fleet Ter-minal** the major cruise operators are represented, making it a good place to peruse what is on offer. Breakfast here at the **Al Porto Café Restaurant** 🍴①, while watching the comings and goings of the waterfront.

A boardwalk hugs the Trinity Inlet shoreline fronting the marina. The two major jetties that embrace the marina are open to all, though it is prohibited to enter the smaller jetties where private craft are moored. Check out the variety of craft or what the fishermen are catching as you wander north along the boardwalk with the

DISTANCE 6.5km (4 miles), not including Red Arrow Circuit
TIME A half-day
START Marlin Marina
END Botanic Gardens
POINTS TO NOTE
Cairns Airport has regular flights direct from most state capitals, and long-distance buses *(see p.108)* connect Cairns with Brisbane and all major stops in between. Queensland Rail (www. traveltrain.com.au) runs a service five times a week between Brisbane and Cairns.

Food and Drink 🍴

① AL PORTO CAFÉ RESTAURANT
1 Spence Street; tel: 4031 6222; daily 7am–3pm; $$
At the wharf end of the Reef Fleet Terminal, Al Porto serves breakfast until they close the doors. There are light tropical-fruit salads, yoghurt and toasted muesli, and eggs several ways with all the extras and steak, pasta, seafood and wine are available for lunch.

Then and Now
When Captain James Cook sailed past in 1770, gingerly negotiating the offshore coral reefs, the hills and coastal flats around present-day Cairns were the home to several tribes of the Djabugay language group, including the Yidinji. Today, local indigen-ous culture is vibrant and celebrated throughout the region.

When to Go
Cairns is blessed with year-round warm temperatures, ranging from 25–33°C (77–91°F), but in summer, humidity is extremely high. It is busiest in the southern states' winter holidays.

Coral Reef Tourism
It all started in 1924 when the Hayles family started taking tourists to Green Island on their trusty vessel, the MV *Merlanda*. The family is also recognised as launching the first glass-bottomed boat.

boats on your right. To the left, the upmarket Shangri-La Hotel occupies the upper floors of **The Pier** complex. An elevated veranda skirts the complex and is home to numerous restaurants and bars. Continue on to **Marina Point**, the location of the **Cairns Yacht Club** and the **Salt House** 🍴②, a huge outdoor restaurant and bar, offering panoramas of the harbour, city and the blue-green hills of Yarrabah.

CAIRNS SWIMMING LAGOON

When you reach the lapping waters of Cairns Harbour, turn left and follow the sweeping path along the shore. At high tide, the water laps the narrow sandy beach; when it recedes, Cairns's famous mudflats are exposed. The mud is a feeding platter for hundreds of water birds, some of which migrate from as far away as Siberia.

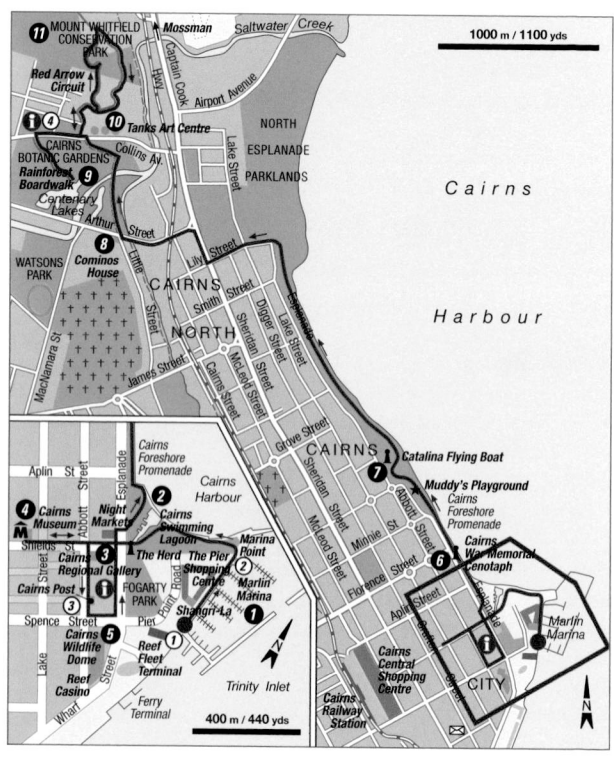

Metal fish spraying water herald the **Cairns Swimming Lagoon** ❷ (Thur–Tue 6am–10pm, Wed noon–10pm). Swimming in the stinger-free clear waters of this vast saltwater pool and lying around on the manicured lawns are virtually mandatory for all visitors, but you might also want to check out *The Herd*, a delightful granite sculpture at the tail end of the lagoon that captures the backs of unidentified animals heading out to sea.

ART GALLERY AND MUSEUM

Cross the **Esplanade** here and head along Shields Street to the **Cairns Regional Gallery** ❸ (corner of Shields and Abbott streets; tel: 4046 4800; www.cairnsregionalgallery.com; Mon–Sat 10am–5pm, Sun 1–5pm; charge). Exhibits include the gallery's collection of international and Australian artists, particularly indigenous and tropical north artists, plus visiting exhibitions.

Walk westwards on Shields Street to the intersection with Lake Street where the **Cairns Museum** ❹ (corner Shields and Lake streets; tel: 4051 5582; Mon–Sat 10am–4pm; charge) occupies the balconied former School of Arts building. Although a typically cluttered regional museum relying entirely on volunteers, the exhibits of Aboriginal history, European and Chinese pioneering in the region and World War II are nonetheless absorbing.

Make your way back along Shields Street and turn right on Abbott Street. On the left-hand side of the street you pass several heritage buildings converted to modern uses: the **Courthouse Hotel** was once the Cairns courthouse, of course, but occupying its 1882 building, the **Cairns Post** still produces the local rags. Turn left at Spence Street to head back to the Esplanade, but not before noting the humble **Oliver's** ⑪③, a fine-dining restaurant where indigenous ingredients and tropical produce are melded with French expertise.

CAIRNS WILDLIFE DOME

On the right is the **Reef Casino**, the top floor of which houses the **Cairns Wildlife Dome** ❺ (tel: 4031 7250;

Above from far left: Swimming Lagoon; the Regional Gallery inside and out.

Food and Drink

② SALT HOUSE MARINA POINT
6/2 Pier Point Road; tel: 4041 7733; www.salthouse.com.au; daily 7–11am, noon–3pm, 6–10pm; $$
The modern design of this large, open-plan restaurant makes the most of its prime waterfront position. Great for breakfast, lunch, or afternoon tapas, it really comes into its own at dinner when steaks and seafood are seared on the immense wood-fired grill. There's live music, and the scene can start pumping at night, particularly towards the end of the week.

③ OLIVER'S
5/63 Abbott Street; tel 4041 1221; www.olivers.net.au; Mon–Sat 6pm–late; $$$
This acclaimed restaurant blends European and Asian styles with fresh seasonal produce and Indigenous ingredients. French chef David Bres' à la carte menu changes every six weeks. Enter from Spence Street.

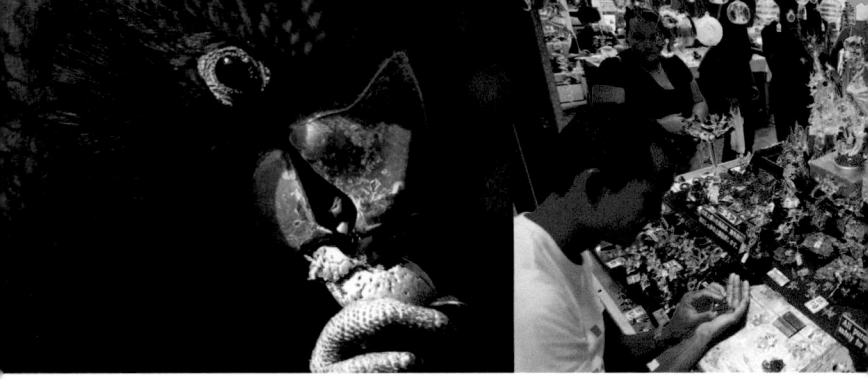

www.cairnsdome.com.au; daily 9am–6pm; charge). Star billing goes to Goliath the 4m (13ft) estuarine crocodile, but there are bird shows, koalas and more. Set aside about an hour – more for feeding times – although remember your ticket is valid for five days so you can return any time.

Turn left at the Esplanade, where you will soon see the helpful **Cairns & Tropical North Visitor Information Centre** (51 The Esplanade; tel: 4051 3588; www.cairnsgreatbarrierreef.org. au Mon–Fri 8.30am–6.30pm, Sat–Sun 9am–6.30pm).

NIGHT MARKETS

Cross over Shields Street, to the **Night Markets** (daily 5–11pm), a raggedy collection of food and merchandise stalls that swings into life at dusk. Cross the Esplanade, skirt the north-western shore of the Lagoon and join the **Cairns Foreshore Promenade**.

Below: Goliath the crocodile at the Cairns Wildlife Dome.

CAIRNS FORESHORE PROMENADE

The promenade hugs the shoreline almost as far as the airport. During the day, shade is available, but scarce, so be prepared. Information panels along the walk describe the history and ecology of the Cairns region. Two artillery pieces flank the **Cairns War Memorial Cenotaph ❻**, erected to commemorate those from Cairns who died in World War I. The clock faces are painted permanently showing 4.28am, the time at which the Anzac landing at Gallipoli began on 25 April 1915.

Continue along the promenade, through **Muddy's Playground**, a wet and wild playground for little kids with a welcome café for a cool drink.

Nearby, atop a tall plinth, is a tiny commemorative model of a **Catalina flying boat ❼**, a frequent visitor to Trinity Inlet during World War II. From their base at Cairns, these remarkable aircraft flew patrols of up to 24 hours in duration, locating and attacking ships of the Japanese fleet.

Pass behind the children's playground pirate ship as the path swings inland and continue north along the Esplanade as it sweeps around to the left and turns into Lily Street. Continue down Lily Street, cross busy Sheridan Street at the lights and turn right, walking one block down Sheridan. Turn left into Arthur Street (which becomes Greenslopes Street), then go over the railway

crossing and Lily Creek bridge.

On the next corner is **Cominos House** ❽ (tel: 4032 1368; Mon–Fri 9am–5pm), a colonial-style home on stilts that was the residence of one of Cairns's earliest settler families until 1988. Relocated from its original Abbott Street site, it has been adapted into an environmental and arts centre.

BOTANIC GARDENS

Opposite and on your right is a path leading into the **Cairns Botanic Gardens** ❾ (tel: 4044 3398; Mon–Fri 7.30am–5.30pm, Sat–Sun 8.30am–5.30pm; free). Enter the shady gardens and cross the narrow foot-bridge over the mangrove-lined Saltwater Creek. Just after the crossing, take the right fork on the path and then the left fork a little further on. The dense bush on your left closely represents the rainforest before European settlement, with huge swamp paperbarks and other native trees (many of them labelled).

You'll soon emerge onto Collins Avenue opposite the **Tanks Art Centre** ❿ (www.tanksartscentre.com; Mon–Fri 9am–4.30pm; free gallery entry), an extraordinary contemporary art and performance facility creatively housed in three massive World War II oil-storage tanks. These three tanks were completed for the Royal Australian Navy in 1944 and camouflaged here to store crude oil for the war effort. In the early 1990s talk of removing the tanks caused an outcry, so it was decided to redevelop the site into this unique and heritage-listed arts space.

If you have the energy, continue up the hill past the tanks to the **Mount Whitfield Conservation Park** ⓫ and the **Red Arrow Circuit** (1.5km/1 mile). There are some steep sections to this track, but the rewards will be walking through virgin rainforest and sweeping views over Cairns and Trinity Bay.

Walking west on Collins Avenue, you soon reach the original Botanic Gardens entrance and the information centre, toilets, orchid house and **Botanic Gardens Restaurant/Cafe** ⓰④, which is the perfect place for lunch. Afterwards you could walk it off on the **Rainforest Boardwalk**, starting opposite the main entrance, through lush tropical rainforest.

Return to the Centre

From here, the best way to return is to catch a bus on Collins Avenue. There is a stop right outside the original entrance. Or wander back through the gardens and catch a bus from Sheridan Street. Otherwise, call a taxi *(see margin, right)*.

Above from far left: red-tailed black cockatoo at the Cairns Wildlife Dome; Night Markets; Catalina flying boat monument.

Local Transport
Within Cairns call 131008 for Black & White taxis or catch Sunbus buses (tel: 4057 7411; www.sunbus.com.au); the Lake Street Transit Centre is the main terminal.

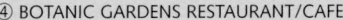

Food and Drink

④ BOTANIC GARDENS RESTAURANT/CAFE
Collins Avenue; tel: 4053 7087; daily 7am–4.30pm; $
Enjoy a light salad, or maybe one of the sinfully sticky waffles, under a canopy of tropical rainforest trees.

KURANDA CIRCUIT

Silently glide over a green sea of tree canopies on the award-winning Skyrail Rainforest Cableway to pretty Kuranda on the lush highlands above Cairns. Kuranda is encircled by rainforest and renowned for arts and crafts and its alternative lifestyle.

Kuranda Conveniently Packaged
Consider combining your Skyrail booking with one of two optional packages: Rainforestation includes the Koala Gardens, amphibious vehicle trip and Aboriginal dance performance; Kuranda Wildlife Experience includes the Koala Gardens, BirdWorld and the Butterfly Sanctuary.

DISTANCE 44.5km (28 miles) of which 3km (2 miles) is on foot
TIME A full day
START Caravonica Terminal
END Freshwater Railway Station
POINTS TO NOTE
Book ahead through your accommodation or directly with Skyrail (tel: 4038 1555; www.skyrail.com. au) or Kuranda Scenic Railway (tel: 4036 9333; www.ksr.com.au). Both offer railway/cableway packages. You can also get bus transfers from your accommodation to either terminal and from one terminal to the other (handy if you self-drive). Book your departure time for 9am; the last train leaves Kuranda at 3.30pm. This tour can also be done by ascending on the railway and returning on the cableway, or just doing a round trip on either the cableway or railway.

Your journey on the **Skyrail Rainforest Cableway** launches from **Caravonica Terminal ❶** (corner of Cairns Western Arterial Road and Captain Cook Highway, Smithfield), a 15-minute drive north of Cairns along the Captain Cook Highway. The 7.5km (5-mile) aerial journey takes approximately 1½ hours, including two informative stops along the way where you can get out and explore the rainforest of **Barron Gorge National Park**.

SKYRAIL RAINFOREST CABLEWAY

As you set off from Caravonica Terminal and skim above the **McAlister Range**, the dense canopy of World Heritage tropical rainforest – the oldest 'old-growth' tropical rainforest on earth, that is home to an amazing diversity of life – stretches out below. The rainforest actually extends over 500km (310 miles) along the north Queensland coastline. Look back for a spectacular view of Cairns out to the Coral Sea. At the first stop, at **Red Peak ❷**, you can join the complimentary **ranger-guided walks** along a short boardwalk surrounded by giant ferns, lush palms and towering trees. Together with interpretive

signs and rainforest displays, the rangers will help you identify some of the rainforest's more interesting and unusual species. Spend at least half an hour here to savour this pristine environment before re-boarding a gondola for the short journey to the second stop.

Barron Falls

At **Barron Falls** ❸ you disembark onto a boardwalk that leads to three lookouts providing breathtaking forest-framed views of the mighty gorge and falls. Especially impressive when the Barron is in full flood during the wet season (Dec–Mar), the flow drastically reduces for the rest of the year. Here you will also find the **Rainforest Interpretation Centre**, with interactive displays, videos and information that will help unravel some of the mysteries of this fascinating ecosystem. Re-board a gondola for the final 10-minute journey over the rainforest and the impressive **Barron River** to Kuranda village.

KURANDA

Skyrail's Kuranda terminal is adjacent to the **Kuranda Railway Station**, from where it is just a short wander along Coondoo Street to heart of quaint **Kuranda village** ❹. It is exceedingly easy to lose 4–5 hours leisurely strolling among the shops, cafés

and wildlife attractions while day-dreaming about moving here permanently! Discovered in the 1960s by hippies who wanted to live an alternative lifestyle in idyllic surroundings, the rainforest village continues to attract legions of talented artists and craftspeople, hence the plethora of bustling markets.

There are plenty of places for a break; stop for coffee and a bagel at the **Windmill Café**, see ⑪① *(p.79)*, or a bit further along Coondoo Street you can lunch beside the rainforest at **Frogs Restaurant**, see ⑪② *(p.79)*. Where Coondoo intersects with

Rainy Days
Do not be put off by rain, as some say this is when the rainforest is at its very best – shrouded in mist and streaked with thundering waterfalls.

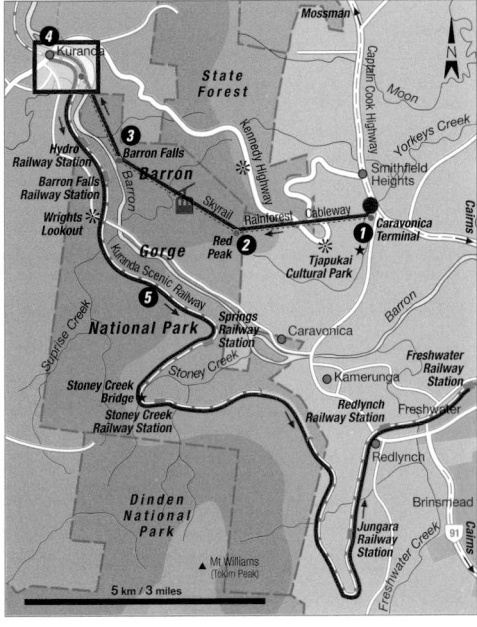

Therwine Street you will see **Centenary Park**, home to the very helpful **Kuranda Visitor Information Centre** (tel: 4093 9311; www.kuranda.org). From here you can start on an easy, one-hour, 3km (2-mile) circuit walk that combines the Jumrum Creek, Jungle Walk and River Walk trails.

Markets

Turn right turn from Coondoo Street and head along Therwine Street. On the right are the **Original Kuranda Rainforest Markets** Ⓐ (corner Therwine and Thooree streets; daily 9am–3pm), a village within a village, with exclusive, locally made fashions, crafts and foods. Diagonally across the road are the **Heritage Markets** (Rob Veivers Drive; www.kuranda markets.com; daily 9.30am–3.30pm), with yet more souvenirs and fashions, but also featuring a couple of wildlife attractions. The market areas overflow with local and imported crafts and produce; kangaroo, toad and crocodile products swamp the sidewalks, and also attract musicians, buskers and fortune-tellers. The rainforest surrounding Kuranda has been home to the Djabugay people for over 10,000 years, making it also a popular spot to pick up a souvenir didgeridoo.

Kuranda Attractions

At the rear of the Heritage Markets is **BirdWorld Kuranda** Ⓑ (tel: 4093 9188; www.birdworldkuranda.com; daily 9am–4pm; charge), home to the largest single collection of free-flying birds in Australia. Over 75 species of the most spectacular birds from all corners of the planet are on display, including Australia's endangered, flightless cassowary.

A walkway links BirdWorld to two more wildlife attractions. The **Australian Butterfly Sanctuary** Ⓒ (8 Rob Veivers Drive; tel: 4093 7575; www.australianbutterflies.com; daily

Below: sampling locally made produce.

10am–4pm; charge) is the largest butterfly enclosure in Australia. The flight aviary is home to some 2,000 tropical butterflies, including the spectacular Cairns birdwing. On the other side of BirdWorld is **Kuranda Koala Gardens** ❿ (tel: 4093 9953; www.koalagardens.com; daily 9am–4pm; charge), where you can get your photo taken cuddling a koala, watch wombats and kangaroos, spot a freshwater crocodile and brave the walk-through snake house.

Back on Coondoo Street you can sample a delicious range of homemade cakes and pastries at **The Coffee Kitchen**, see ⑪③.

KURANDA SCENIC RAILWAY

Make your way back to Kuranda Railway Station for the 3.30pm departure of the **Kuranda Scenic Railway** ❺, a 90-minute journey through deep ravines and lush rainforest and past spectacular waterfalls. Constructed between 1882 and 1891, the railway is a tremendous engineering feat. On-board commentary reveals the trials and tribulations involved in its construction. Hundreds of men were employed to build the 15 hand-dug tunnels and 37 bridges, and at least 23 workers died before the railway opened up the rich Atherton Tablelands to agriculture and later to tourism.

There is a brief photo stop at the station overlooking **Barron Falls** to see the river plunge (or trickle, depending on the time of year) from its placid Kuranda reaches into the gorge. The train also slows over a picturesque steep gully as it crosses **Stoney Creek Bridge**, with a backdrop of one of the region's most spectacular waterfalls. Eventually you will arrive at **Freshwater Railway Station** to catch your transfer bus back to Cairns or the Skyrail terminal.

Food and Drink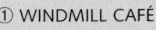

① WINDMILL CAFÉ
25 Coondoo Street; tel: 4093 9466; daily 9am–4pm; $
Conveniently located on the corner as you walk up the hill from Skyrail, this welcoming café serves up a startling array of tasty bagels and sandwiches, luscious cakes and coffee, and freshly squeezed juices.

② FROGS RESTAURANT
11 Coondoo Street; tel: 4093 7405; www.frogsrestaurant.com.au; daily 10.30am–4pm; $$
Built in 1923, and one of Kuranda's first cafés, this licensed restaurant with superb rainforest views has an extensive menu ranging from gourmet pizzas to fresh local barramundi.

③ THE COFFEE KITCHEN
20 Coondoo Street; tel: 4093 9169; daily 7.30am–5pm; $
Grab a table inside or out under a tree and choose from an assortment of freshly baked, handmade baguettes, pastries and cakes.

Above from far left: walking through the rainforest village of Kuranda; spectacular view of the Kuranda Scenic Railway.

More Critters
The Australian Venom Zoo (8 Coondoo Street; tel: 4093 8905; www.tarantulas.com.au; daily 10am–4pm; charge) breeds and displays venomous spiders, snakes and insects. Venom is extracted for biomedical research purposes, while some dangerous critters are bred for the pet trade. BatReach (Jungle Walk, Coondoo Street; tel: 4093 8858; Tue–Fri and Sun 10.30am–2.30pm; admission by donation) is a volunteer-operated rescue and rehabilitation centre for injured and orphaned flying foxes

PORT DOUGLAS AND MOSSMAN GORGE

Travel north from Cairns along one of Australia's most spectacular coastal roads as it clings to a stunning coastline with dramatic views of the Coral Sea. Discover the seaside towns of Port Douglas and Palm Cove, and float in the crystal-clear waters of Mossman Gorge.

DISTANCE 182km (113 miles)
TIME A full day
START/END Cairns
POINTS TO NOTE

You will need a car for this trip *(see p.108)*, and don't forget your swimming gear. This tour can be combined with tour 13 *(see p.84)*; Daintree village is a 35km (22-mile) drive north of Mossman.

Food and Drink

① **BREAKFAST WITH THE BIRDS**
Rainforest Habitat Wildlife Sanctuary, corner Captain Cook Highway and Port Douglas Road; tel: 4099 3235; www.rainforest habitat.com.au; daily breakfast 8–10.30am; $$$
Enjoy a full buffet breakfast with fruits, pastries, cereals and hot food from the BBQ while immersing yourself in the wetlands environment and being joined by a throng of birds that wander freely amid the tables.

Tjapukai
Only 15 minutes north of the city of Cairns, Tjapukai Cultural Park (Cairns Western Arterial Road, Smithfield; tel: 4042 9900; www.tjapukai. com.au; daily 9am–5pm, evening show 7–10pm; charge) is ensuring the 40,000-year-old Tjapukai culture remains alive. Be led through a Dreamtime journey of creation with traditional dance, music and legends. You can also learn how to play a didgeridoo, throw a boomerang and start a fire with sticks.

This journey past Cairns's northern beaches unveils golden swathes of palm-fringed sand along a 26km (16-mile) stretch of unspoilt tropical shoreline fronting the Coral Sea and backed by rainforest-clad mountains. Small, laid-back villages, mixing residential with low-key tourism development, rest lazily beside the sea. Further on, the larger, glitzier towns of Palm Cove and Port Douglas lure an eclectic crowd of backpackers, botoxed and bling-adorned retirees and a few well-heeled international visitors.

TO PORT DOUGLAS

Make an early start from Cairns and head north on the Captain Cook Highway for 67km (41 miles) to Port Douglas. As you leave Cairns you will pass the **Skyrail Rainforest Cableway** *(see p.76)* to Kuranda and **Tjapukai Cultural Park** *(see margin, left)*. Branching off the highway to the east are roads leading to serene beachside villages such as **Yorkeys Knob**, **Trinity Beach** and **Ellis Beach**, as well as

Palm Cove *(see p.83)*. Just before the last, look out for the **Cairns Tropical Zoo** *(see margin, right)*. Be sure to pause at **Rex Lookout** to take in the panoramic views.

Rainforest Habitat Wildlife Sanctuary

Just before the entrance to Port Douglas is the **Rainforest Habitat Wildlife Sanctuary ❶** (Corner Captain Cook Highway and Port Douglas Road; tel: 4099 3235; www.rain foresthabitat. com.au; daily 8am–5pm; charge), where you can enjoy **Breakfast with the Birds**, see ⑪①, and after breakfast there are presentations on the local ecology of wetlands, rainforest and grasslands.

PORT DOUGLAS

From here it is only 6km (4 miles) to the heart of **Port Douglas ❷** (or Port, as it's known to the locals). Not very long ago, Port Douglas was a sleepy seaside settlement. Today, it has been transformed into a fashionable tropical holiday resort, with the whole spectrum of tourist accommodation, award-winning restaurants, beautiful galleries and upmarket shopping. Fortunately, the transition has not entirely robbed Port Douglas of its natural charm.

The approach from the main road is lined by an avenue of about 450 huge African oil palms; as many again are planted around the **Sheraton Mirage Resort** and the **Marina Mirage**. They

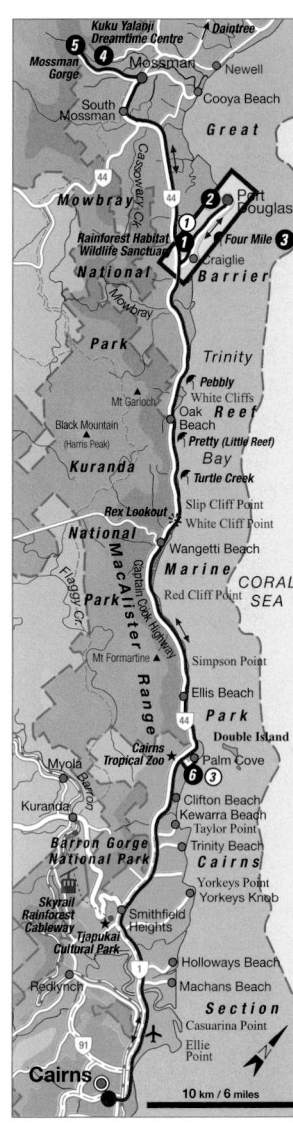

Above from far left: wandering the Mossman Gorge; Port Douglas.

Cairns Tropical Zoo
Only 20 minutes' drive north of Cairns, the excellent Cairns Tropical Zoo (Captain Cook Highway, Palm Cove; tel: 4055 3669; www.cairnstropical zoo.com.au; daily 8.30am–4pm; charge) offers a huge range of animal-related activities throughout the day, including crocodile-feeding, free-flight bird shows and snake shows. Apart from these regular events, the zoo offers close-up encounters, such as koala cuddling, within its 6ha (15 acres) of landscaped tropical gardens.

form part of the extravagant vision of former multi-millionaire Christopher Skase, who transplanted the trees here at a cost of about A$1,500 each. Skase went spectacularly bust in a series of media and leisure ventures in the late 1980s: happily, Port Douglas fared better and has continued to prosper.

Macrossan Street

The main drag, **Macrossan Street**, is lined with a colourful array of shops,

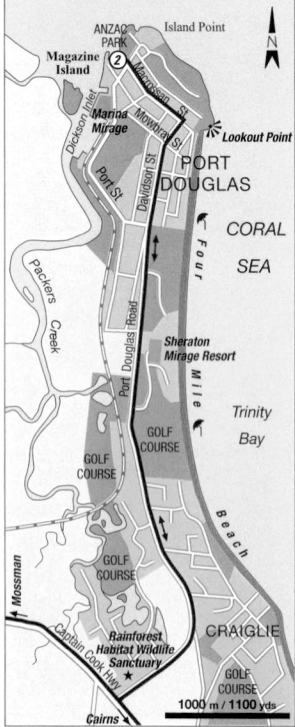

eateries and restaurants and well worth a wander. The sidewalks are thronged with casual pedestrians, who seem to have all the time (and money) in the world. With a core population of approximately 4,000 people, the town also sports a world-class marina and international-standard golf courses.

At the western end of Macrossan Street (on the corner with Wharf Street), the Court House Hotel is the oldest pub in town (in operation since 1878) and is now home to **The Wharf Street Bistro**, see ⑪②, famed for its hearty pub meals and great live entertainment in the evenings. Across the road is **Anzac Park**, which overflows with market stalls on Sunday mornings (8am–midday), selling arts and crafts as well as fresh fruit and vegetables.

Four Mile Beach

Running along the southeastern side of the peninsula, **Four Mile Beach** ❸ is the town's prime asset, a long, lonely stretch of sand, backed by palm trees, with no signs of development (accommodation and houses are neatly hidden behind the palms). Swimming is safe, but during stinger *(see p.29)* season (Oct–May), stay inside the stinger nets.

TO MOSSMAN GORGE

Take the main road out of Port Douglas back to the Captain Cook Highway. Turn right for the 26km (16-mile) drive north to Mossman. As

you climb up towards the misty mountains shrouded in greenery, the air becomes cooler and filled with the refreshing scent of the rainforest. Turn left at Mossman and follow the signs for 5km (3 miles) to Mossman Gorge.

On the way to the gorge is the **Kuku Yalanji Dreamtime Centre ❹** (tel: 4098 2607; www.yalanji.com.au; Mon–Fri 8.30am–5pm, Sat 8.30am–1pm). The Kuku Yalanji are the indigenous inhabitants of this land, which stretches from around Cooktown in the north to near Chillagoe in the west and Port Douglas in the south. The centre's free Aboriginal Art Gallery is well worth a browse. They also offer 90-minute guided walks (charge) around Mossman Gorge, visiting culturally significant sites, sharing dreamtime legends and providing an insight into their traditional relationship with this unique tropical environment.

MOSSMAN GORGE

Make your way to the car park for spectacular **Mossman Gorge ❺**. Remember to put on your swimming gear if you want to experience the crystal waters of the Mossman River; swimming here is safe as long as you exercise caution. The short **River Circuit track** (10 minutes) takes you to a viewing platform over the river, but if you would like to go on a longer walk and escape the crowds, take the 3km (2-mile) **Rainforest Circuit track** (approximately one hour return).

PALM COVE

Head back along the Captain Cook Highway towards Cairns. After about 50km (31 miles) turn left for **Palm Cove ❻**, a beachside development (some might say overdevelopment) where the brick-cobbled streets and 500-year-old melaleuca trees bestow a wonderfully tranquil mood. With its exclusive hotels and resorts, resaurants and spas, this spot is about sheer relaxation, pampering and fine-dining. For afternoon tea overlooking the sea, try **Ando's Bar & Grill**, see ⑪③. From here it is a 30-minute drive back to Cairns on the Captain Cook Highway.

Above from far left: lemur at Cairns Tropical Zoo near Palm Cove; peaceful Palm Cove scene; the Kuku Yalanji Dreamtime Centre offers guided walks around Mossman Gorge.

Food and Drink

② THE WHARF STREET BISTRO
Court House Hotel, Corner Wharf and Macrossan Streets, Port Douglas; tel: 4099 5181; www.at-the-courty.com; daily 11.30am–9.30pm; $$
Renowned for having the best steaks in town, so order your favourite cut from the grill. Other temptations from the extensive menu include BBQ pork spare ribs and the Coral Sea curry, a Thai-style seafood curry. This pub has atmosphere, entertainment and clientele spilling out onto the pavement and balconies.

③ ANDO'S BAR & GRILL
6/139 Williams Esplanade, Palm Cove; tel: 4059 2234; daily 7am–10pm; $$
A divine setting with a great outlook over the Coral Sea, Ando's is all about relaxed dining. Just enjoy a coffee or cool drink in the sea breeze, savour one of their delicious pizzas or tackle the popular Reef and Beef classic meal.

DAINTREE AND CAPE TRIBULATION

Take a full day to drive through the spectacular Wet Tropics and Daintree World Heritage area. Spot crocs on the river, wander boardwalks through forest and mangroves, take a dip at Mason's swimming hole and enjoy long, sprawling, deserted beaches.

River Cruise

You will need to leave Cairns by 7am to make it comfortably to the Daintree River for a 10am river cruise. Operators include: Crocodile Express (tel: 4098 6120; www.daintree connection.com.au), the first operator on the river in 1979, which offers daily one-hour cruises 8.30am–5pm); Bruce Belcher's Daintree River Cruises (tel: 4098 7717; www. daintreerivercruises. com.au; daily one-hour cruises 8.15am–4pm); and Chris Dahlberg's Daintree River Tours (tel: 07 4098 7997; www. daintreerivertours. com.au; daily two-hour dawn cruise).

DISTANCE 44km (27 miles)
TIME A full day
START Daintree
END Cape Tribulation
POINTS TO NOTE

Daintree is 110km (68 miles) north of Cairns via Mossman; alternatively, this route could easily be linked with the Port Douglas and Mossman Gorge tour *(see p.80)*. A car is needed for this tour *(see p.108)*, and you will need to bring cash to pay for the ferry. Consider overnighting in the rainforest *(see p.116)* to maximise your wilderness experience with adventures such as nocturnal wildlife walks *(see margin, opposite)* and surfing the jungle canopy. Book your morning Daintree River cruise in advance *(see margin, left)*.

The Daintree River is one of the longest rivers on the Australian East Coast and named by George Elphinstone Dalrymple after his friend Richard Daintree, an English geologist. Dalrymple wrote 'No river in North Australia possesses surroundings combining so much of distant mountain grandeur with local beauty and wealth of vegetation.'

DAINTREE

Daintree ❶ is a tiny, historic village on the southern bank of the scenic Daintree River overlooked by Queensland's third-highest mountain, **Thornton Peak** (1,374m/ 4,507ft). It's a picturesque setting, originally the base for cedar-getters who came to log prized red cedar, which once flourished in the area. There's not much more here to detain you otherthan the **Daintree Village General Store**, see ⑪①, which can supply you with information on the area and sell tickets for a Daintree River Cruise if you have not already booked.

River Cruises

Daintree River cruises *(see margin, left)* take place on different sections of

the river. The tours take you up or downstream, through narrow reaches lined with mangroves and rainforests that are rich in wildlife. It is unusual not to spot a crocodile from a safe distance, especially in the cooler months when the huge reptiles leave the water to sun themselves on the riverbank. The departure jetty for many of the river cruises is a short downhill stroll from the Daintree Village General Store.

Afterwards, for an early lunch, return 3km (2 miles) back down the road you came in on from Cairns, taking a right turn into the **Daintree Eco Lodge and Spa** *(see p.116)*, nestled into the rainforest, for the **Julaymba Restaurant**, see ①②, with its gallery displaying authentic Aboriginal artefacts and artworks.

Daintree Ferry

Drive east along Daintree Road for 10km (6 miles) to the turnoff to the **Daintree Ferry ❷** (6am–midnight; charge). On the other side of the two-minute crossing, a good sealed road tunnels through overhanging trees all the way to Cape Tribulation. Take care on the narrow, winding stretches that hug the cliff edges. Speed bumps are placed along the road to slow traffic in areas where southern cassowaries – large, flightless birds *(see p.94)* that can be very aggressive towards humans – may be encountered. Cassowaries undertake a key role in the rainforest,

spreading tree seeds after they have digested the fruit.

After 8km (5 miles) you reach the **Alexandra Range Lookout**, with sweeping views back to the south, across the wide mouth of the Daintree River, to Snapper Island and the sugar-cane fields and ranges beyond.

Daintree Discovery Centre

A little further north, pull over at the **Daintree Discovery Centre ❸** (tel:

Above from far left:
Daintree River;
the ferry.

Croc Country
Crocodiles are an important part of north Queensland's wetlands, freshwater and marine areas, living mainly in tidal reaches of rivers, as well as in freshwater sections of lagoons, swamps and waterways, and along some beaches and offshore islands. Crocodiles are most active at night and during the breeding season (Sept–Apr). Always heed crocodile warning signs.

Above from left:
elevated view of Cape Tribulation; experiencing the rainforest from a zipline.

Food and Drink 🍴

③ CAFÉ-ON-SEA
90 Cape Tribulation Road,
Thornton Beach; tel: 4098 9118;
daily 9am–5pm; $$
Situated under swaying trees, overlooking the Coral Sea, where the rainforest meets the reef, this casual, licensed café offers cakes, muffins and biscuits for morning and afternoon tea or salad, burgers and a perfectly grilled barramundi for more substantial appetites.

4098 9171; www.daintree-rec.com. au; daily 8.30am–5pm; charge). This award-wining interpretive centre provides a self-guided rainforest booklet and comprehensive audio guides that give an excellent insight into what you see from the low-impact boardwalk and the breathtaking heights of the Canopy Tower. At 23m (76ft) in height, and featuring five viewing platforms, the tower provides a fantastic experience for photographers, botany enthusiasts and birdwatchers alike.

TO CAPE TRIBULATION

Drive further north, passing the **Cow Bay Hotel Motel** and then **Thornton Beach,** where you can stop for a stroll along this peaceful stretch of sand backed by dense rainforest. You can walk to the mouth of **Cooper Creek,** one of Australia's richest mangrove ecosystems (but watch out for crocodiles), while **Café-On-Sea,** see 🍴③, provides the perfect beachside break.

Continue north to reach the **Marrdja Boardwalk ④,** a short 30-minute loop walk beside a running rocky stream, through lush rainforest and mangroves. A little further north again is **Mason's Café, Store and Tours** (Cape Tribulation Road; tel: 4098 0070; www.masontours.com.au), which offers guided day and night walks, 4WD tours and croc-spotting. If you want to cool down, a little path

behind the store leads to **Mason's swimming hole,** a lovely spot where you can rope-swing into the cool water of Myall Creek.

CAPE TRIBULATION

It is just a short drive from Mason's Café to the final destination of the tour, **Cape Tribulation ❺**. The cape was so named by Captain Cook in 1770 because 'all his troubles began here'. Just after the 'Welcome to Cape Tribulation' sign, turn right into the **Dubuji Visitor Area** and walk the easy 1km (⅔-mile) boardwalk loop around freshwater swamps and mangroves, which also has access to the expansive **Myall Beach**.

Cape Tribulation consists only of a small cluster of shops, including a pharmacy, small supermarket and PK's Jungle Village, a backpackers' resort with a rowdy bar. Continue 1km (⅔ mile) north to **Kulki–Cape Tribulation Beach,** where there is an easy pathway to an elevated lookout over Cape Tribulation Beach and a rough track over the headland to Myall Beach. These two magnificent, picture-postcard beaches, where golden sands and azure waters rim the deep-green rainforest, are the main drawcard and the climax of the drive. Do not be alarmed by the harmless goannas (large monitor lizards) which hang out here scavenging from picnickers.

For the adventurous, **Jungle Surfing Canopy Tours** (Cape Tribulation; tel: 4098 0043; www.junglesurfing.com. au; daily 7.45am–3.30pm; charge) offer an exhilarating way to experience the rainforest on flying-fox ziplines, stopping at five tree platforms to take in the bird's-eye views.

From here, the road north is unsealed and only accessible by 4WD. It is approximately 2½ hours' drive from Cape Tribulation to Cairns.

Cape to Coral
From the Daintree/ Cape Tribulation area it is only 30–40 minutes by boat to the Great Barrier Reef. Snorkelling and diving trips are run by Ocean Safari (tel: 4098 0006; www. oceansafari.com.au) and Rum Runner (tel: 1800 644 227; www. rumrunner.com.au).

Old-Growth Rainforest

The tropical rainforest stretching from just north of Cairns through Cape Tribulation and on to Cooktown is around 110 million years old, and a remnant of the extensive forest that used to cover most of Australia and, before that, Gondwanaland. With this extraordinary ancestry, the north Queensland rainforest boasts the highest number of endemic species in the world, and is rightfully recognised and protected within the Wet Tropics World Heritage Area. Some of the most accessible rainforest is in the Daintree National Park, showcased by the Daintree Discovery Centre (see p.85), a short distance north of the Daintree ferry.

ATHERTON TABLELANDS

Discover the charm of the Atherton Tablelands, also known as the Cairns Highlands, on this two-day drive visiting a plateau of patchwork farms, volcanic lakes and tumbling waterfalls. On the way, sample some of the world's best coffee in Mareeba and overnight in historic Yungaburra.

Landscape Oddity
As you drive through this part of Queensland, you will see the landscape is characterised by the presence of large termite mounds.

DISTANCE Day one to Yungaburra: 120km (75 miles); day two: 70km (44 miles)
TIME Two days
START Cairns
END Crawford's Lookout
POINTS TO NOTE
You will need a car (see p.108), and to stay overnight in Yungaburra (see p.117). For Kuranda see tour 11. Instead of returning to Cairns at the end of the tour, you could carry on to Mission Beach or visit some of the sights en route to Cairns on that tour (see p.94).

Below: Davies Creek National Park.

The Tablelands have long been known as the food bowl of the Tropics. Incorporating the townships of Mareeba, Atherton, Herberton, Ravenshoe, Millaa Millaa and Malanda, the region is renowned for its dairy products and for growing tea, coffee and sugar. Combine this bountiful larder with the invigorating natural beauty of fast-flowing waterfalls, pristine lakes and crystal streams, and you have a destination that revitalises the five senses.

TO MAREEBA

Leave Cairns nice and early and head north for 13km (8 miles) on the Captain Cook Highway to the Smithfield roundabout. Take the road to Kuranda *(see p.77)*, on the Kennedy Highway. It is a 30-minute winding drive through dense rainforest. Follow the signs to Mareeba where the vegetation suddenly changes from rainforest to 'dry bush'. The change is brought about by two factors: less rainfall and different soil. This heralds the beginning of the Atherton Tablelands: rich, rolling country, much of which is cultivated for agriculture.

Davies Creek National Park

After crossing Davies Creek, take the road on the left that leads to the **Davies Creek National Park ❶**. This road is unsealed for 7km (4 miles) but passable with a conventional vehicle. The creek winds and falls through a granite gorge, providing the opportunity to take a quick dip in the dozens of rocky plunge pools. Beyond the campground there is a 2km (1¼-mile) walk to lookouts above **Davies Creek Falls**, and a short circuit track leads to a sandy picnic area where platypus may be spotted in the adjacent creek.

Head back out onto the Kennedy Highway, where the bush soon gives way to open farmland with mango, citrus and avocado orchards.

MAREEBA

Mareeba is the centre of Australia's major coffee-growing region, with over 75 percent of Australia's crop grown in the district's fertile soils. Before you enter the town, about 5km (3 miles) from the Davies Creek turnoff, billboards direct you to **Jaques Coffee Plantation ❷** (tel: 4093 3284; www.jaquescoffee.com). It is a 4km (3-mile) detour along Gilmore Road and well worth the effort for an insight into the coffee industry. Take a 20-minute tour (charge), followed by a coffee- or liqueur-tasting, or just sample the produce at **Jaques Coffee Plantation Café**, see ⑪①.

Back on the highway, proceed into the town of **Mareeba**, where the **Coffee Works Experience** (136 Mason Street; tel: 4092 4101; www.coffeeworks.com.au) offers a coffee gift shop, coffee-tasting and the **Courtyard Café**, see ⑪②. Tea-drinkers are also catered for!

TO ATHERTON

Mareeba played a major role in the success of the Battle of the Coral Sea during World War II; as you head south out of town on the Kennedy Highway there are a couple of historic collections. The first, after 5km (3 miles), is **Beck's Museum ❸** (tel: 4092 3979; daily 10am–4pm; charge), the largest privately owned collection of war machines, planes and equipment in Queensland. Almost opposite is **Warbird Adventures** (Mareeba Airport; tel: 4092 2391; www.warbirdadventures.com; Wed–Sun 10am–4pm) where, for

Above from far left: view of the Tablelands around Mareeba; sampling the wares at the Coffee Works Experience.

War History With the outbreak of World War II, the entire Atherton Tablelands area became the largest military base during 1943–1945, supporting between 100,000 and 300,000 troops from 140 different units.

Food and Drink

① JAQUES COFFEE PLANTATION CAFÉ & COFFEE SHOP
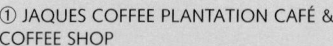
137 Leotta Road, Mareeba; tel: 4093 3284; www.jaquescoffee.com; daily 9am–5pm; $
Accompany the local brew with a selection of cookies, scones and cake, including tropical fruit cheesecakes.

② THE COFFEE WORKS COURTYARD CAFÉ
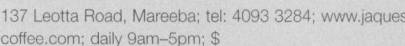
136 Mason Street, Mareeba; tel: 4092 4101; www.coffeeworks.com.au; daily 9am–4pm; $
As well as superb coffee, the café offers light lunches, sweet treats, gourmet sorbet and superb gelati.

a price, you can take to the skies in one of several ex-military aircraft. Helicopter flights are also available.

Continue your journey southwards towards **Walkamin**. Just before the town, the **Mount Uncle Distillery** (1819 Chewko Road; tel: 4086 8008; www.mtuncle.com; daily 10am–5pm) bottles and sells premium liqueurs and spirits distilled from tropical products such as coffee, limes and macadamia nuts. In the tiny township of Tolga, the **Tolga Woodworks Gallery and Café**, see ⑪③, has quite a reputation for home-style cooking and great coffee, as well as its crafts and furniture carved from rare and beautiful local timbers.

ATHERTON

Just five minutes down the road from Tolga is the town of **Atherton ❹**. The **Atherton Information Centre** (corner Main Street and Silo Road; tel: 4091 4222; www.athertontinformationcentre.com.au; daily 9am–5pm) provides maps and brochures and makes accommodation bookings. One of the town's attractions is the **Crystal Caves** (69 Main Street; tel: 4091 2365; www.crystalcaves.com.au; daily Mon–Fri 8.30am–5pm, Sat 8.30am–4pm, Sun 10am–4pm; charge), where a simulated cave houses a fine collection of crystals and fossils.

Curtain Fig Tree

From Atherton, follow the signs for Malanda and Herberton, then take a left turn where the signpost indicates

that it's 12km (7 miles) to Yungaburra. As you approach town, detour right to the **Curtain Fig Tree ❺**. Walk along the boardwalk that surrounds the tree and an interpretive display explains how this amazing natural sculpture was formed; a draped curtain of aerial roots first grew from the parasitic fig, 'strangling the host tree', the whole thing then fell sideways and the fig lowered its roots to the ground.

YUNGABURRA

Yungaburra ❻ is a historic village that has changed little since 1910 and boasts no fewer than 18 heritage-listed buildings. It makes a good restful overnight base, and the **Yungaburra Visitor Centre** (Cedar Street; tel: 4095 2416; www.yungaburra.com; daily 10am–6pm) can help with booking accommodation and dining options such as atmospheric **Nick's Swiss-Italian Restaurant and Yodeller's Bar**, see ⑪④, and the romantic **Eden House Retreat and Mountain Spa**, see ⑪⑤.

Crater Lakes National Park

Just to the east of town is **Lake Eacham**, a sparkling blue lake in a drowned volcanic crater fringed by lawn and surrounded by rainforest. Along with Lake Barrrine, it is the main feature of **Crater Lakes National Park ❼**, and the perfect spot for an afternoon swim and sunbathe.

If you would like to stretch the legs, there is an easy 3km (2-mile) circuit around the lake. This is also a bird-watcher's paradise, with over 180 recorded species.

About 5km (3 miles) further north-east along the Gillies Highway is Lake Eacham's twin, **Lake Barrine**. The **Lake Edge Teahouse Restaurant**, see ⑪⑥ *(p.93)*, is an ideal breakfast spot for the second day of this tour. After breakfast consider joining the **Lake Barrine Rainforest Cruise** (tel: 4095

Above from far left: Yungaburra; tranquil Lake Barrine.

Food and Drink

③ TOLGA WOODWORKS GALLERY AND CAFÉ
Kennedy Highway, Tolga; tel: 4095 4488; www.tolgawoodworks.com.au; daily 9am–5pm; $$
They make the most of locally grown produce, so try the Greek, Thai or Tuscan summer salads, along with breads and cakes and baked in a wood-fired oven and finish off with local coffee or leaf tea.

④ NICK'S SWISS-ITALIAN RESTAURANT AND YODELLER'S BAR
33 Gillies Highway, Yungaburra; tel: 4095 3330; www.nicksrestaurant.com.au; Tue–Sun 11.30am–3pm and 5.30–11pm. Wed 11.30am–3pm; $$$
Choose from Nick's extensive Swiss-Italian menu, including pasta, rosti and Swiss bratwurst. Or if you prefer modern Australian, go with crumbed crocodile fillets or a jackaroo sirloin steak.

⑤ EDEN HOUSE RETREAT AND MOUNTAIN SPA
20 Gillies Highway, Yungaburra; tel: 4095 3355; www.edenhouse.com.au; Tue–Sat 6–10.30pm; $$$
This exquisite and romantic retreat also offers great dining in a heritage-listed dining room or in the delightful tropical gardens. Local produce such as mangoes, avocados, redclaw crustaceans and grass-fed beef feature on the menu.

3847; www.lakebarrine.com.au; charge). You will be able to spend 45 minutes cruising around the volcanic crater, listening to an informative wildlife commentary and sighting pelicans and other water birds, tortoises, fish and maybe – in the cooler months – amethystine pythons, the world's third-largest snake (up to 8.5m/28ft long) sunning themselves on branches. For good birdwatching and walking, there is a 5km (3-mile) track around the lake. A short stroll away from the restaurant are the giant twin kauri pines, estimated to be 1,000 years old.

Above: 100 percent Australian coffee; Nerada Tea.

MALANDA

From Lake Eacham, take the road south to **Malanda**, amid lush green pastures over red volcanic soil. The black-and-white Friesian cows grazing in these pastures each produce up to 30 litres (6½ gallons) of milk a day! The **Malanda Dairy Centre** (8 James Street; tel: 4095 1234; daily 9.30am–4pm; charge) runs factory tours (Mon–Fri before noon) and serves up a seriously good milkshake. If, after yesterday's focus on coffee, you are interested in finding out how tea is grown and processed, call into the **Nerada Tea Visitor Centre** (tel: 4096 8328; www.neradatea.com.au; daily 9am–4pm), just 10km (6 miles) outside of Malanda on the Glen Allyn Road. Back on the Malanda–Millaa Millaa Road, consider stopping at **Tarzali Lakes Aquaculture Centre** for the **Smokehouse Café**, see ⑪⑦.

MILLAA MILLAA AND THE WATERFALL CIRCUIT

Continue along the highway for about 15km (9 miles) through farmland and rainforest to **Millaa Millaa ❽**, another dairy town, ringed by some of the Tablelands' most spectacular waterfalls. Enter the **Waterfall Circuit** by taking the Theresa Creek Road, 1km (⅔ mile) east of Millaa Millaa on the Palmerston Highway. The first stop is **Millaa Millaa Falls**, considered to be the perfect 'drop' of water and used in many shampoo commercials. Drive onto **Zillie Falls** (viewed from above) and **Ellinjaa Falls**.

Coffee in Queensland

Over 75 percent of Australia's Arabica coffee crop is grown in the rich, fertile district around Mareeba on more than a dozen large plantations. Tropical north Queensland was recognised as ideal coffee country as early as the 1880s, and by 1900 over 50 farmers were producing coffee in the Cairns Highlands. Queensland beans even won acclaim in Europe. The industry then declined for several decades as it struggled to remain financially viable, before re-emerging in the 1980s centred around Mareeba. Modern harvesting and processing technology, Australian's rapidly escalating addiction to quality espresso, and the burgeoning café culture have underpinned today's success story.

Detour to Ravenshoe

From Millaa Millaa you could detour southwest 25km (15 miles) on the Old Palmerston Highway to **Ravenshoe** ❾, Queensland's highest town at 920m (3,000ft). The **Ravenshoe Visitor Centre** (24 Moore Street; tel: 4097 7700; www.ravenshoevisitor centre.com.au; daily 9am–4pm) can help with accommodation bookings and information on regional waterfalls and bushwalks. Within the visitor centre is also the **Nganyai Interpretive Centre**, showcasing the culture of the local Jirrbal people, whose language is one of the oldest spoken in the world.

RETURN TO CAIRNS

Homeward bound, take the Palmerston Highway east towards Innisfail. After 5km (3 miles) turn left on Brooks Road to **Mungalli Falls**. At the **Mungalli Creek Dairy** (251 Brooks Road, Millaa Millaa; tel: 4097 2233; www.mungallicreekdairy.com.au; daily 10am–4pm) you can sample organic milk and cheese, and snack at the café. Brooks Road loops back to the Palmerston Highway, which descends through 14km (8 miles) of lush rainforest. At **Crawford's Lookout** ❿ there are views through a clearing down to the North Johnstone River, where you may spot white-water rafters. Here too is **Mamu Rainforest Canopy Walkway** (Wooroonooran National Park; tel: 4064 5294; www.

derm.qld.gov.au/parks/mamu; daily 9.30am–5.30pm; charge), where you can perch high amongst the rainforest canopy, looking down at the mighty North Johnstone River. These rainforest-clad mountains have cultural significance to the Mamu Aboriginal people, and informative signs explain the cultural history of the area. The return walk is 2.5km (1½ miles), but count on at least an hour to enjoy the scenery properly along the 350m (1,150ft) of elevated walkway and from the 37m (120ft) observation tower with two viewing decks.

From here head 25km (16 miles) east to the Bruce Highway, where it's a straightforward run north for 87km (54 miles) back to Cairns. Alternatively, drive south for Mission Beach *(see p.94).*

Above: Mungalli Falls.

Food and Drink 🍴

⑥ THE LAKE EDGE TEAHOUSE RESTAURANT
Lake Barrine, Gillies Highway, Yungaburra; tel: 4095 3847; www.lakebarrine.com.au; daily 9am–5pm; $$
Overlooking the lake, this place serves hearty breakfasts, light lunches, such as soups, salads and sandwiches, and all-day Devonshire teas.

⑦ SMOKEHOUSE CAFÉ
Tarzali Lakes Aquaculture Centre, Malanda–Millaa Millaa Road, Malanda; tel: 4097 2713; www.tarzalilakes.com; daily 10am–5pm; $$
Nestled on the shores of a lake stocked with barramundi, golden perch, jade perch and red claw (a delicious crustacean), it comes as no surprise that this café specialises in freshly prepared fish and, of course, a wide range of smoked treats; more surprising, however, is the extensive Thai menu.

MISSION BEACH
AND DUNK ISLAND

The first day of this driving tour south of Cairns takes you through swaying fields of sugar cane, visiting pristine plunge pools and picturesque waterfalls on the way to the seaside village of Mission Beach. Day two is spent relaxing or enjoying watersports on the tropical paradise that is Dunk Island.

DISTANCE 157km (97 miles) from Cairns to Mission Beach
TIME Two days
START Cairns
END Dunk Island
POINTS TO NOTE
A car is needed. On the first day pack water and a morning snack to enjoy en route at one of the scenic waterfalls. Mission Beach has accommodation options for all budgets, and Dunk Island has camping and a resort *(see p.117)*.

Endangered Cassowary

Mission Beach is one of the few places where visitors are likely to see the southern cassowary, an unusual and endangered bird. This flightless bird is Australia's largest rainforest animal and can reach 2m (over 6ft) in height. Cassowaries are shy, but when disturbed, they are capable of inflicting serious injuries with their three-toed feet that sport a dagger-like claw. They have been known to kick humans with their powerful legs, so be warned: never approch a cassowary.

As you travel south from Cairns, the route passes through spectacular mountain scenery and fertile fields of bananas and sugar cane to reach Australia's wettest towns. It is known as part of the 'Great Green Way', and you will encounter ever-increasing tropical greenery and the relaxed north Queensland lifestyle, where farming and fishing are dominant ways of life and where you can have a yarn with locals in an old Queensland pub.

TO MISSION BEACH

Set out early from Cairns, travelling south on the Bruce Highway through Edmonton and Gordonvale, where the Mulgrave Sugar Mill has been in operation since 1896. **Babinda**, about 60km (37 miles) south of Cairns, competes annually with Tully and Innisfail for the 'Golden Gumboot Award', which goes to the town recording the highest annual average rainfall, usually around 5m (over 15ft). The locals will tell you it rains for 11 months, and drips off the trees for the rest of the year. In fact, large amounts of rain tend to fall in a very short time, and there is plenty of tropical sunshine to power the unusually lush and diverse vegetation.

Babinda Boulders

At Babinda, turn right and follow signs west for 8km (5 miles) to **Babinda Boulders ❶**, a Wet Tropics World Heritage Reserve with visitor facilities, located in the foothills of **Bartle Frere**, Queensland's highest mountain at 1,622m (5,300ft). Take

your bathers to the Boulders and walk the 850m/yd **Wonga Track Rainforest Circuit** to clear pools amidst giant tree ferns, moss-covered boulders and towering trees. The short **Devils Pool Walk** is another lovely stroll through the rainforest to viewing platforms and cascading pools. This entire area is a popular swimming spot for locals and tourists, but stick to the marked swimming areas and exercise care, as there have been drownings at Devils Pool.

Josephine Falls

Continue south on the Bruce Highway, and after 9km (5½ miles) take a right turn to **Josephine Falls ❷**. This is an 8km (5-mile) detour from the highway and 10 minutes' walk through the rainforest to be rewarded by some of the most beautiful falls in Queensland. The tumbling icy waters have been used in many television commercials, and you can take a swim here.

Innisfail and Paronella Park

The sugar town of **Innisfail** is another 13km (8 miles) further south. Sitting at the junction of the North Johnstone and South Johnstone rivers, Innisfail is the no-fuss service hub for the region. From Innisfail, take the Old Bruce Highway (Japoonvale Road) for 18.5km (11½ miles) to **Paronella Park ❸** (Mena Creek; tel: 4065 0000; www. paronellapark.com.au; daily 9am–

7.30pm (guided walks every 30 minutes 9.30am–4.30pm, night tour 6.15pm); charge). Back in 1913 Jose Paronella dreamt of building a Spanish castle alongside Mena Creek, and by 1935 his dream had been realised. A magnificent castle with grand staircase, lakeside tunnels and

Above from far left: idyllic Mission Beach; Paronella Park.

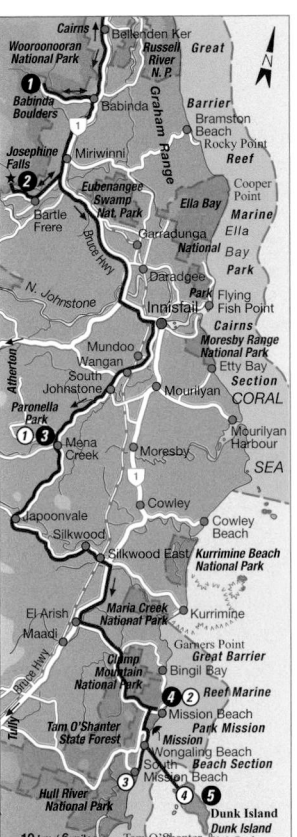

Skydiving

Throughout the day in Mission Beach you may hear shrieks from above; it is just another planeload of skydivers, seeking out the extreme by jumping from 4,260m (14,000 ft). Coming in to land on the glistening sands of Mission Beach makes this one of the most spectacular drop zones in the country. Check out Jump the Beach (tel: 1800 444 568; www.jumpthe beach.com.au), if you too want some serious thrills.

bridges, picnic areas and surrounded by gardens was opened to the public. This is a unique spot to enjoy lunch at **Café on the Deck** ♨①, overlooking Jose's exotic creation.

MISSION BEACH

From Paronella Park, you are about 45 minutes from Mission Beach. Follow the signs south through Japoonvale to Silkwood on the Bruce Highway (23km/14 miles). Turn right onto the highway for **El Arish**, from where you turn left off the highway for the 16km (10-mile) drive to **Mission Beach ❹**. Made up of four communities – **Bingil Bay**, **Mission Beach** itself, **Wongaling Beach** and **South Mission Beach** – it boasts 14km (9 miles) of unspoilt palm-fringed coastline overlooking more than 20 tropical offshore islands dotting the Coral Sea. The area offers a large array of adventure activities, and you will find accommodation for all budgets *(see p.117)*, or book ahead to stay on Dunk Island (www.dunk-island.com).

Call in at the **Mission Beach Visitor Centre** (Porter Promenade; tel: 4068 7099; www.missionbeach tourism.com; Mon–Sat 9am–4.45pm, Sun 10am–4pm), located on the beachfront just outside Mission Beach village on the way to Bingil Bay. There is information on numerous activities, galleries and accommodation options as well as details on the local mascot, the rare and endangered southern cassowary *(see margin, p.94)*. Being the closest mainland point to the Great Barrier Reef, snorkelling and scuba-diving trips are popular and offer a much quieter and less crowded option than the ones offered in Cairns.

White-Water Rafting

Near Tully, in a remote part of the Wet Tropics World Heritage Rainforest, the Tully River snakes through dramatic gorges. Its energy can be experienced on a full-day white-water rafting trip. Along its twisting, scenic descent there are over 45 churning (normally grade 3–4) rapids to conquer on a day packed with action and adventure. No prior experience is necessary, as river guides have intimate knowledge of every bend, curve and drop of the river and rapids. Trips with two main operators, RnR White Water Rafting Adventure (tel: 4041 9444; www.raft.com.au) and Raging Thunder (tel: 4030 7990; www.ragingthunder.com.au), are available year-round with transfers from/to your accommodation in Mission Beach, Cairns, Northern Beaches and Port Douglas. You need to be 13 years or older to raft.

Eating Options

For a sleepy seaside town, Mission Beach has a surprising selection of

sophisticated restaurants and eateries. The **Oceania Bar & Grill**, see ⑪②, offers a relaxing dining experience, while for a romantic dinner with a stunning view, try the **Elandra Restaurant and Bar**, see ⑪③, in South Mission Beach. Here the owner has created an exotic theme of 'safari by the sea'. Even if you do not feel like eating, you can feast your eyes on the collection of tribal arts and artefacts from across the globe.

DUNK ISLAND

Offshore, the Family Group of Islands beckon, with the most northerly, **Dunk Island ❺**, just 4km (2½ miles) out to sea, being the main attraction. To get there, you can take the South Mission Beach Road to the **water taxi** (Banfield Parade, Wongaling; tel: 4068 8310; www.missionbeachwatertaxi.com; six departures daily) for the ten-minute crossing. Note that in order to board, you need to wade through shallow water. Or take the Quick Cat ferry (Clump Point jetty; tel: 4068; www.quickcatcruises.com.au; four departures daily). **Coral Sea Kayaking** (2 Wall Street, South Mission Beach; tel: 4068 9154; www.coralseakayaking.com) offer guided kayak trips to the island, including lunch and leisure time.

Dunk is a beautiful rainforested island, predominately National Park, offering 13km (8 miles) of walking track through most of the island's many habitats, guided horse rides and

lovely secluded beaches. The resort and the main beach, however, is bustling with folks participating in activities such as kayaking, water-skiing, tube rides and wake-boarding. Jet-ski tours around the island are also popular, as is a round of golf on the scenic nine-hole golf course.

The casual **Jetty Café**, see ⑪④, refuels energetic day-trippers with coffee, cool drinks and snacks.

Above: view from Dunk Island.

Food and Drink

① CAFÉ ON THE DECK
Paronella Park, Japoonvale Road (Old Bruce Highway), Mena Creek; tel: 4065 0000; www.paronellapark.com.au; daily 9am–5pm; $
Enjoy a light lunch on the outdoor deck consisting of sandwiches, foccacias, pies or their celebrated homemade jam and scones.

② OCEANIA BAR & GRILL
52 Porter Promenade; Mission Beach; tel: 4088 6222; daily noon–late; $$
In the heart of Mission Beach village, this welcoming bar and kid-friendly restaurant is perfect for a casual dinner. Fresh local seafood and succulent steaks are accompanied by a varied wine list and, of course, icy-cold beer on tap.

③ ELANDRA RESTAURANT AND BAR
Explorer Drive, South Mission Beach; tel: 4068 8154; www.elandraresorts.com; daily 7am–9pm; $$$
Sitting high on a cliff edge where rainforest meets the sea, enjoy modern Australian cuisine with an Asian influence, such as seared king scallops, drunken chicken or a warm Asian noodle salad.

④ JETTY CAFÉ
Dunk Island; tel: 1300 38 4403; www.dunk-island.com; daily 9am–4pm; $$
Offering ultra-casual beachside dining, this little café on the jetty doles out burgers, fish and chips, and seafood baskets to hungry day-trippers.

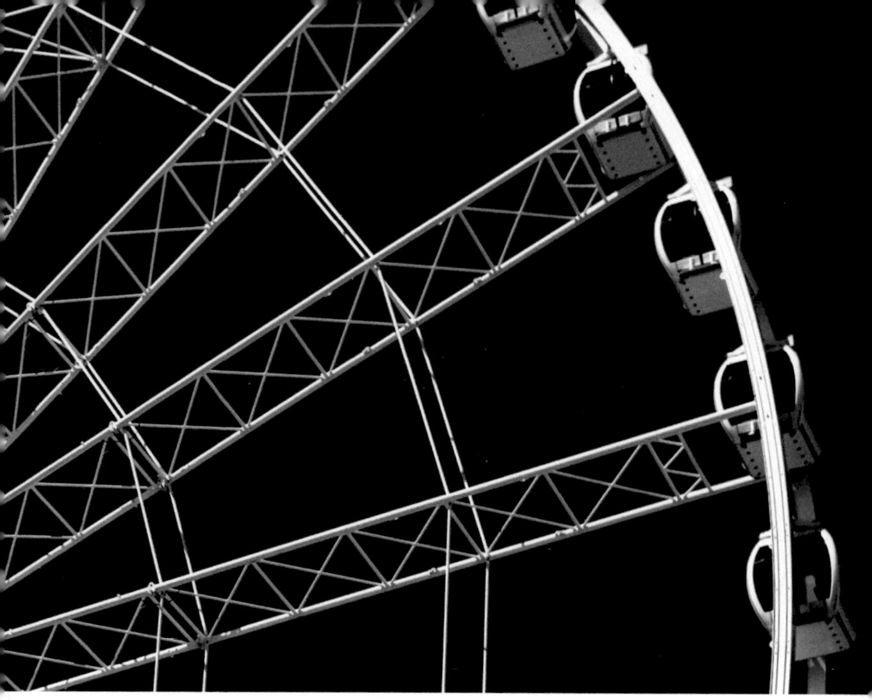

DIRECTORY

A user-friendly alphabetical listing of practical information, plus hand-picked hotels and restaurants, clearly organised by area, to suit all budgets and tastes. Select nightlife listings are also included here.

A

AGE RESTRICTIONS

In Queensland the age of consent for heterosexual sex is 16. For homosexual sex it is 18. Drivers must be 17 to obtain a provisional driving licence, and the legal drinking age is 18.

B

BUDGETING

Accommodation. A bed at a backpacker hostel can be as little as A$25 a night, and a room in a three-star hotel is usually around A$100. A room in a four- or five-star hotel can start as low as A$200, although internet and low-season deals can halve even this tariff.

    Airport taxi. A taxi from Brisbane Airport to central Brisbane will cost around A$50. From Cairns Airport to central Cairns costs about A$18. Train and/or bus options are also available.

    Buses and ferries. A single (2-hour) ticket that allows travel on Brisbane's buses, trains and ferries within one zone costs A$3.40. For the whole day it costs A$6.80.

    Car rental. Renting a small car costs from A$45 per day; a 4WD will cost A$100-150 per day. Petrol (gasoline) costs around A$1.20 per litre.

    Dive courses. Prices range from A$600–900 for courses that include open-water diving on day trips; more expensive courses include on-board accommodation and meals.

    Restaurants. A main course in a budget restaurant costs about A$15, A$20–5 at a moderate restaurant, and A$30–5 at an expensive restaurant. A bottle of Australian wine from a bottle shop (liquor store) starts at about A$8; the same bottle in a restaurant is likely to cost A$18, hence the popularity of BYO (Bring Your Own) restaurants. A glass of house wine averages around A$8. A 'pot' of full-strength draught beer *(see margin, p.17)* costs from A$3.50, and a cup of espresso coffee or tea about the same.

C

CLOTHING

In subtropical Brisbane, dress is informal and casual, though some hotels, restaurants and clubs will require a jacket and tie in the evening. Lightweight clothing is suitable year-round, but bring something warm in case the temperature drops at night, especially in autumn and winter. In Cairns's tropical climate, dress is always informal, with very few restaurants and clubs requiring a jacket and tie. Lightweight clothing is suitable all year round, but again bring something warm for cool winter nights in the highlands. To protect yourself against sunstroke and sunburn, you should

wear suncreeen, a broad-brimmed hat, and a shirt with collar and sleeves. Bring swimwear and good sunglasses for the beach.

CRIME AND SAFETY

Brisbane, Cairns and the Gold Coast are fairly safe, but do not leave valuables unattended or in parked cars. Avoid dark, empty spaces and public toilets at night, and be aware of the potential of alcohol-fuelled violence around nightclubs. The police are helpful and competent.

CUSTOMS

Non-dutiable allowances are 250g (8oz) of tobacco goods (approximately a carton of cigarettes) and 2,250ml (a quart) of beer, wine or spirits, and other dutiable goods to the total value of A$900, plus personal clothing, footwear and toiletries. Up to A$450-worth of dutiable goods, not including alcohol or tobacco, are allowed in the baggage of children under 18. Visit www.customs.gov.au for further information.

Strict quarantine regulations forbid the importation of foods, plants, animals and their by-products. Heavy jail penalties apply to the smuggling of drugs of any kind. Visitors are allowed to carry up to four weeks' supply of prescribed medications, but for larger supplies you should carry a doctor's certificate for customs purposes.

DISABLED TRAVELLERS

A useful booklet, *Accessible Queensland*, and information on other support services (available Mon–Fri) can be obtained from the Disability Information Awareness Line (DIAL), tel: 3224 8444 in Brisbane, or toll-free outside Brisbane on 1800 177 120.

ELECTRICITY

Electrical power is 240/250v AC, 50Hz Universal. Most hotels also have outlets for 110v (shavers only). Adaptors for Australian power outlets are readily available at the airport and in shops and hotels.

EMBASSIES AND CONSULATES

The following are the closest contacts for travellers needing assistance when in Queensland.

British Consular Agency, Level 26 Waterfront Place, 1 Eagle Street, Brisbane; tel: 3223 3600; http://ukinaustralia.fco.gov.uk

Canadian Consulate General, Level 5, 111 Harrington Street, Sydney; tel: 02 9364 3000; recorded information: 02 9364 3050; www.canada.org.au

Travelling with Kids
Coastal Queensland is one big playground, from theme parks on the Gold Coast to koala-cuddling at Australia Zoo and Cairns Tropical Zoo, to snorkelling on a coral reef. The Queensland Museum and Wheel of Brisbane on Brisbane's South Bank are sure to please, and at Tjapukai Aboriginal Cultural Park in Cairns the daily shows include an evening of corroboree around a fire. Child-concession admission usually applies to children 12 years and under, but it can be as old as 16. Check the *Yellow Pages* directory for professional babysitting services.

Carbon-Offsetting

Air travel produces a huge amount of carbon dioxide and is a significant contributor to global warming. If you would like to offset the damage caused to the environment by your flight, a number of organisations can do this for you, using online 'carbon calculators', which tell you how much you need to donate. In the UK travellers can visit www.climatecare. org or www. carbonneutral.com; in the US log on to www.climatefriendly. com or www. sustainabletravel international.org

Consulate General of Ireland, Level 26, 1 Market Street, Sydney; tel: 02 9264 9635; www.irishconsulates sydney.net

US Consulate General, MLC Centre, Level 10, 19–29 Martin Place, Sydney; tel: 02 9373 9200; after-hours emergencies, tel: 02 4422 2201; http://Sydney.usconsulate.gov

EMERGENCY

In an emergency, dial 000 for police, fire or ambulance services.

GAY AND LESBIAN TRAVELLERS

Queensland may not be the gay mecca that you would find in Sydney, but there is a thriving gay community in the state's capital, and Noosa is a favoured spot to wind down after the Sydney Gay Mardi Gras in March.

To find the rainbow edge to Brisbane's nightlife, try The Wickham Hotel (www.thewickham.com.au) in Fortitude Valley or Spring Hill's Sportsman Hotel (www.sportsman hotel.com.au), the oldest gay bar in town. Brisbane's Pride Festival (www.brisbanepride.org.au) is held each June. The highlight of the month-long festival is generally a parade and fair day.

Check out the gay press for futher information; *Queensland Pride* is a free monthly newspaper, and *Q News* is a free fortnightly newspaper; both are based in Brisbane. Gay and Lesbian Tourism Australia (www.galta. com.au) promotes gay-friendly tourism operators.

GREEN ISSUES

Queenslanders take environmental issues seriously, particularly in the heavily populated coastal regions. For information on how climate change threatens the Great Barrier Reef, see www.gbrmpa.gov.au/corp_site/key_issues/climate_change. Recycling of glass, paper, aluminium and certain plastics is widespread; look for recycling bins with yellow lids. For more information see www.climatesmart.qld.gov.au.

HEALTH

Australia has excellent medical services. For medical attention out of working hours go to the casualty department of a major hospital or, if the matter is less urgent, visit one of the medical clinics in the major towns and tourist centres. Look under 'Medical Centres' or 'Medical Practitioners' in the *Yellow Pages*, or ask at your hotel.

Healthcare and Insurance

Citizens of countries with which Australia has a reciprocal agreement (UK,

Above: lifeguards at Noosa.

Ireland, Finland, Norway, Sweden, Malta, Netherlands, New Zealand) are allowed restricted access to government Medicare service; this covers free care as a patient in hospital and subsidised medicines. It does not cover dental care, ambulance costs or emergency evacuation to your home country, so you are advised to take out your own travel insurance. Visitors from other countries should have private insurance to cover all medical care. See www.health.gov.au for details.

Inoculations

No vaccinations are necessary for entry into Australia unless you have visited an area (including parts of South America and Africa) infected by yellow fever, cholera or typhoid in the previous 14 days.

Natural Health Hazards

The biggest danger for travellers in Australia is the sun. Even on mild, cloudy days it has the potential to burn. Wear a broad-brimmed hat and, if you are planning on being out for a while, a long-sleeved shirt made from a light fabric. Wear SPF 30+ sunblock at all times, even under a hat.

Apart from stingers *(see p.29)*, the main danger in north Queensland coastal waters are saltwater (or estuarine) crocodiles. Do not enter waters where crocodile warning signs are posted, always ask for local advice, and if in doubt do not venture in.

Pharmacies and Hospitals

'Chemist shops' are a great place to go for advice on minor ailments such as bites, scratches and stomach trouble. They also stock a wide range of useful products such as sunblock, nappies (diapers) and non-prescription drugs. If you have a prescription from your doctor, and you want to take it to a pharmacist in Australia, you will need to have it endorsed by a local medical practitioner.

HOURS AND HOLIDAYS

Business Hours

Core business hours are Mon–Thur 9am–5.30pm, Fri until 9pm in the cities, Sat 9am–1pm. However, retailers tend to follow demand, and hours vary widely, with most shops in tourist precincts open on Saturday afternoon and Sunday.

Public Holidays

Banks, post offices, government and private offices close on the following holidays:

New Year's Day (1 Jan)
Australia Day (26 Jan)
Good Friday (date variable)
Easter Monday (date variable)
Anzac Day (25 April)
Labour Day (First Monday in May)
Queen's Birthday (2nd Monday in June)
Christmas Day (25 Dec)
Boxing Day (26 Dec)

Internet Facilities

Internet cafés have proliferated in recent years, and travellers to Australia should have no trouble finding internet access in major cities and tourist locations. Many hotels and hostels now have facilities for people travelling with their own laptops, and local libraries fill the gap in communities where there is no commercial internet facility.

L

LEFT LUGGAGE

At Brisbane Airport there are left-luggage facilities in the international terminal but not in the domestic terminal. Cairns Airport has a baggage-storage facility run by Smart Carte Australia (tel: 0407 359 678). There are lockers for luggage on all levels of Brisbane's Transit Centre at Roma Street. To check the facilities available at other Queensland train stations, see www.traveltrain.com.au.

M

MAPS

The accredited Visitor Information Centres, indicated by the yellow 'i' against a blue background, give away useful maps of their areas. The Queensland Holidays website carries a map of Queensland showing the locations of the Visitor Centres. Visit the RACQ Travel Centres (www.racq.com.au) for touring maps. They can also be mailed overseas to international visitors.

MEDIA

Print and Online Media

Brisbane's daily newspaper is the *Courier-Mail* (www.couriermail.com.au), a lively tabloid published Monday to Saturday. On Sunday the major Brisbane newspaper is the *Sunday Mail*. Both are part of the News Corporation stable. In Cairns the local daily is the *Cairns Post* (www.cairns.com.au).

Australia has two national papers, the *Australian* (www.theaustralian.com.au) and the *Financial Review*, and foreign-language newspapers and magazines are available at newsagents in Brisbane, the airport and major tourist districts.

Radio and Television

The Australian Broadcasting Commission (ABC) runs national television channels as well as an extensive network of radio stations. ABC television offers excellent news and current affairs, as well as local and imported drama, comedy, sports and cultural programmes. The commercial TV stations, Channels 7, 9 and 10, offer news, drama, soaps, infotainment, travel shows and, between them, coverage of all the major international sporting events. Many hotels provide access to a large number of cable television stations.

Radio stations include Triple J (107.7 FM in Brisbane and 107.5 in Cairns), rock and comment for the twentysomethings; Classic FM (106.1 FM in Brisbane and 105.9 FM), continuous classical music; and Radio National (792 AM and 105.1 FM in Cairns), excellent national news and events coverage. Commercial radio stations include Triple M

FM (104.7 in Brisbane) for popular local and international rock, and Nova 1069 for contemporary music (106.9 FM).

Of particular interest to overseas travellers is Australia's ethnic/multicultural broadcaster, SBS. The organisation's television channel offers many foreign-language films and documentaries, and Australia's best coverage of world news. SBS Radio (93.3 FM in Brisbane) offers programmes in a variety of languages.

MONEY

The four major banks in Australia are ANZ, Commonwealth, National Australia and Westpac. Trading hours are generally Mon–Thur 9am–4pm and Fri 9am–5pm.

Cash Machines

Most bank branches have automatic teller machines (ATMs) that are networked with Cirrus, Maestro and other networks, allowing you to access funds from overseas accounts.

Credit Cards

Most establishments display a list of the credit cards they will accept, usually including MasterCard and Visa, and less so Amex, Diners Club and JCB.

Currency

Australia's currency is the dollar (A$), which is divided into 100 cents. Notes come in denominations of 5, 10, 20, 50 and 100 dollars, each of which has a distinctly different colour. Coins come in denominations of 5, 10, 20 and 50 cents (silver-coloured), and one and two dollars (bronze-coloured). The one dollar coin is, confusingly, larger than the two. Shopkeepers usually round up change to the nearest five cents.

Taxes

The Australian government collects a 10 percent goods and services tax (GST) on virtually all retail sales. Under a 'tourist refund scheme', the GST on goods valued at over A$300, bought from the same shop within the previous 30 days and carried as hand luggage, can be recovered upon leaving the country at a Tourist Refund Scheme (TRS) booth located beyond customs at the airport; you must have retained the tax invoice.

Tipping

Tipping is not customary even for taxi drivers and restaurant staff, but it is not unusual to reward good service with a gratuity of up to 10 percent of the bill. Hotel staff do not solicit or expect tips, but certainly will not be offended by one.

Travellers' Cheques

All well-known brands can be exchanged at banks, five-star hotels and exchange bureaux.

Above from far left: the *Cairns Post* has been the city's local rag for well over a hundred years; Queen Street Mall in Brisbane.

Lost Property

Report loss or theft of valuables to the police immediately, as most insurance policies insist on a police report. In Brisbane, lost property found at a Citytrain station is held for three days at that particular station before being forwarded to Roma Street Station (tel: 3235 1859 Mon–Fri 10.15am–2.25pm. For anything left on Brisbane's ferries, tel: 3229 7778, daily 9am–5.30pm. To locate property left on a Brisbane bus, contact the Brisbane City Council call centre, tel: 3403 8888. The lost-property office is located at 69 Ann Street, Brisbane.

P

POLICE

In an emergency call 000. At other times call the local police station, which can be located on www.police.qld.gov.au

POST

Post offices are open Mon–Fri 9am–5pm; some post shops are also open Sat 9am–noon. The Brisbane GPO (261 Queen Street) is open Mon–Fri 7am–6pm. The main post office in Cairns is at 13 Grafton Street (Mon–Fri 8.30am–5.30pm). Post offices will hold properly addressed mail for visitors and sell stamps, standard and Express Post envelopes and packaging. Post boxes are red (standard mail) or yellow (Express Post).

The cost of overseas mail depends on the weight and size of the package. To send a postcard to Europe or the USA costs A\$1.40. A letter up to 50g in weight will cost A\$2.10.

S

SMOKING

In Queensland it is illegal to smoke inside restaurants, bars and clubs, including commercial outdoor eating or drinking areas, at patrolled beaches and major sports stadiums. Additionally, it is illegal to smoke in a car carrying children under the age of 16.

T

TELEPHONES

The international code for Australia is 61 and the area code for Queensland is 07. Within Queensland, you do not need to dial this code.

To call from Australia, dial 0011 + country code + area code (drop the first 0) + number. The country code for Canada and the US is 1, Ireland is 353 and the UK is 44.

There are plenty of public telephones and most take phone cards. All Australian coins can be used in payphones, though many public phones only use phone cards, which can be bought in general stores, post offices and newsagents. For eight-figure numbers, you dial the 07 area code only if you're calling from outside Queensland. For Directory Assistance, dial 1223.

Mobile (Cell) Phones

The GSM 900 mobile phone system network in Australia is compatible with systems everywhere except Japan and the Americas. To use your mobile here for a short term you should buy an Australian SIM card with prepaid calls. Providers include Telstra (www.telstra.com), Optus (www.optus.com.au) and Virgin Mobile (www.virginmobile.com.au).

TIME ZONES

Queensland operates on Australian Eastern Standard Time (Greenwich Mean Time plus 10 hours). Daylight saving is not observed in Queensland, but does apply, from different dates, in the other states across three time zones, giving, at worst, up to six differing times across the country.

TOURIST INFORMATION

Before you leave home, see the Tourism Australia website, www.australia.com. Queensland is well served by organisations designed to help visitors. In addition to information centres, the following websites will answer almost any questions that you might have: www.experiencequeensland.com; www.queenslandholidays.com.au

The main tourist information centres in Queensland are:

Brisbane
Corner Albert and Queen streets; tel: 3006 6290; www.ourbrisbane.com, and the Southern Queensland Visitors Information Centre, Level 2, Brisbane International Airport; tel: 3406 3190; www.southernqueensland.com.au

Cairns
Tourism Tropical North Queensland; 51 The Esplanade; tel: 4051 3588; www.tropicalaustralia.com.au

Gold Coast
Cavill Avenue, Surfers Paradise; tel: 1300 309 440; www.verygoldcoast.com

Mission Beach
Porters Promenade; tel: 4068 7099; www.missionbeachtourism.com

Noosa
Hastings Street, Noosa Heads; tel: 5447 4988; www.tourismnoosa.com.au

Whitsunday Coast
Tourism Whitsundays; Bruce Highway, Proserpine; tel: 4945 3711; www.whitsundaytourism.com

TRANSPORT

Airports

Many international airlines provide regular links between Brisbane Airport (www.bne.com.au) and Europe, the US and Asian and Pacific nations. Frequent Qantas and Virgin Blue domestic services fly to Brisbane and Coolangatta (www.goldcoastairport.com.au) from Sydney, Melbourne, Canberra and other state capitals.

Brisbane Airport's adjacent international and domestic terminals are connected by shuttle bus. Few hotels provide regular courtesy coach transfers, but some will do so on request. Cabs to the city are expensive. However, a combination of comfortable, regular Airport Commuter coaches and a fast shuttle train takes you to and from the central city terminal at Roma Street with shuttles from there to many of the downtown hotels. Translink (tel: 131230; www.translink.com.au) can provide all the travel

Public Transport
Translink (tel: 131230; www.translink.com.au) is responsible for public transport by bus, train and ferry transportation throughout the region.

information you need. A cab ride to the central business district costs about A$15.

Cairns Airport (www.cairnsairport.com) has regular air links to Asia and the Pacific as well as to Brisbane, Sydney and Melbourne. The airport is 8km (5 miles) from central Cairns. Many hotels provide coach transfers, or Sun Palm's Express Coaches (tel: 4087 2900; www.sunpalmtransport.com) cost A$10 to Cairns hotels. Airport Connection (tel: 4099 5950; www.tripshuttle.com) services Port Douglas, Mission Beach and Cape Tribulation.

Rail and Long-Distance Bus

Brisbane's main rail terminal is the Transit Centre in Roma Street, a short taxi ride to/from most Brisbane hotels. Fast trains travel to Robina on the Gold Coast, from 4am to 11pm, at half-hour intervals most of the day, every hour during less busy times. The *Sunlander* rail service (three times weekly) along the coast from Brisbane to Cairns takes about 31½ hours. The faster *Tilt Train* (twice weekly) takes just over 24 hours. Contact Queensland Rail's Traveltrain Holidays (tel: 1300 132 722; www.traveltrain.com.au).

Coaches to Surfers Paradise, Southport and other Coast destinations are provided by Surfside Buslines (www.surfside.com.au). Both Greyhound Australia (www.greyhound.com.au) and Premier Motor Service (www.

premierms.com.au) service all the major resort towns along the East Coast between Brisbane and Cairns; the direct journey between the two cities takes 29 hours.

Taxis

Taxis showing a light can be flagged down from the kerb. Rates per km are around A$1, plus an A$4 initial charge. A small phone booking fee is charged if you call a cab, and most cabs take credit cards. Taxis normally carry only four passengers, but maxi-cabs, which take six to 10 passengers, are available on request at 1½ times normal rates. Smoking is banned in all cabs, and the passenger may be fined if not wearing a seatbelt. To book a cab (just about anywhere in Australia!) call tel: 131 008.

Car Rental

International car-hire companies offer good discounts on pre-booked hires, with the option to return the vehicle to another major centre at no extra charge. The minimum age for hiring a car is 18, but drivers under 25 pay a surcharge. A national driving licence is acceptable if it is written in English; otherwise you should obtain an international driver's licence. If your picture id is not on the licence, you may have to produce your passport. Insurance on conventional rental cars is invalid on unsealed (dirt) roads, but most hire companies insure 4WD vehicles for any road that is shown on a map.

Cover for single-vehicle accidents is subject to a high excess payment. Major international car-rental firms include:

Avis (tel: 13 63 33; www.avis.com.au)

Budget (tel: 1300 362 848; www.budget.com.au)

Europcar (tel: 1300 131 390; www.europcar.com.au)

Hertz (tel: 13 30 39; www.hertz.com.au)

Thrifty (tel: 1300 367 227; www.thrifty.com.au).

Driving

Traffic drives on the left in Australia, so you usually give way to the right and road signs usually match international rules. There is a 0.05 percent blood alcohol limit for drivers, which is widely enforced by the practice of random breath tests. Police also conduct random drug tests.

Off-road Driving

When driving on sand it is always advisable to carry a 'snatch strap' in the event of getting bogged in loose sand. Check with your 4WD hire company that you have one in your vehicle. Also consult them for the correct tyre pressure for your vehicle. Lowering pressure in your tyres makes driving on sand safer and easier. However, do not forget to re-inflate your tyres once again when driving on bitumen. Also note that speed limits are signposted and enforced.

V

VISAS AND PASSPORTS

Your passport must be valid for at least six months from your date of arrival. All non-Australian citizens need a valid visa to enter Australia, with the exception of New Zealand citizens travelling on New Zealand passports, who are issued with a visa on arrival in Australia. Visas are available from Australian visa offices such as Australian embassies, high commissions and consulates, and from travel agents and airlines in some countries.

The **Electronic Transfer Authority** (ETA) enables visitors to obtain a visa on the spot from their travel agent or airline office. The system is in place in over 30 countries, including the US. ETA visas are generally valid over a 12-month period; single stays must not exceed three months, but return visits within the 12-month period are allowed. ETAs are issued free, or you can purchase one online for A\$20 from www.eta.immi.gov.au.

Most EU citizens are eligible for an **eVisitor** visa, which is free and can be obtained online. **Tourist visas** are available for continuous stays longer than three months, but must be obtained from an Australian visa office, such as an embassy or consulate. A A\$20 fee applies. Those travelling on any kind of tourist visa are not permitted to work while in Australia.

Useful Websites

Cairns & Tropical North Visitor Information Centre (www.cairnsgreat barrierreef.org.au), Tourism Queensland (www.queens landholidays.com. au); Brisbane City Council (www. ourbrisbane.com).

Coastal Queensland has a huge range of accommodation options, and you are unlikely to have difficulty finding a place to stay unless there's a major event in progress. When booking hotel accommodation, there is some latitude for striking a deal for longer stays, weekend rates, standby rates and so on. Check for internet-only rates, and it is always worth asking about 'specials' when speaking directly to the hotel. Many hotels have rooms for non-smokers; request these when booking. Do not be afraid to ask to inspect a room before you make your decision.

Brisbane

Banana Bender Backpackers

118 Petrie Terrace; tel: 3367 1157; www.bananabenders.com; $

Only a short bus ride from the city centre, this popular hostel has a range of room options, including female-only dorms and double and twin rooms. The fan-cooled rooms are kept clean, and Bananas also offer airport shuttle service, internet access and backpacker party nights.

Brisbane City YHA

392 Upper Roma Street; tel: 3236 1004; www.yha.com.au; $

This convenient hostel is close to the Brisbane Transit Centre and to Caxton Street's fabulous nightlife. Rooms are either three-share or doubles, and all are air-conditioned.

There's a good café, rooftop pool, games room full of electronic games, and a very helpful travel and tour desk.

Brisbane Marriott

515 Queen Street; tel: 3303 8000; www.marriott.com.au; $$$$

The five-star Marriott boasts state-of-the-art business facilities in its luxury rooms, plus excellent views. There is a pool, spa and health club, and it's an easy stroll to the riverside restaurant precincts of Riverside Centre and Eagle Street Pier.

Chifley at Lennons

66 Queen Street; tel: 3222 3222; www.chifleyhotels.com.au; $$$

This 20-storey tower is located right in the city's heart, opposite Myers in the Queen Street Mall. There are 152 units plus suites, including entire non-smoking floors, a restaurant, bar and a heated outdoor swimming pool.

Comfort Inn and Suites Northgate Airport

186 Toombul Road, Northgate; tel: 3256 7222; www.choicehotels.com; $$$

The Comfort Inn is the closest motel to Brisbane's airport, with good facilities such as babysitting, restaurant, bar, laundry and internet. It is also very convenient if you have a car, being far from traffic and parking problems. Rooms are very comfortable, at the top end of motel accommodation.

Lucerne on Fernberg

23 Fernberg Road, Paddington; tel: 3369 6686; www.lucerne.net.au; $$

A heritage-listed B&B in what is believed to be the oldest privately owned building in Queensland. The beautifully presented accommodation is in the separate coach house or the cottage; both with mini home-theatre systems and cooking facilities. BBQ, parking and laundry facilities are available, and guests are welcome to enjoy the lovely wraparound veranda and gardens.

The Marque

103 George Street; tel: 3221 6044; www.marquehotels.com; $$$

Less than five minutes' walk to the city, casino or the river, the Marque is a modern boutique hotel with excellent service and three grades of rooms. The top-of-the-range spa suites overlook the river and South Bank. Facilities include a heated outdoor pool, gymnasium, restaurant and bar, and undercover parking.

Rydges Southbank Hotel

9 Glenelg Streets, Southbank; tel: 3364 0800; www.rydges.com.au/southbank; $$$–$$$$

Location, location, location. Right near the South Bank Parklands and cultural precinct, with hundreds of rooms ranging over several categories, this five-star hotel can have great-value room deals on the internet. There are bars and restaurants, but you also have the great restaurants on Grey and Little Stanley streets nearby.

The Sebel and Citigate King George Square

At Ann and Roma streets; tel: 1800 777 123 (reservations), 3229 9111; www.mirvachotels.com; $$$

Right opposite King George Square, close to the river and central shopping district, these two adjacent towers share the same management and contact details. The Sebel is the slightly pricier of the two, but both are good value with a very central location and excellent facilities including parking, pool, restaurants and bar.

Stamford Plaza Hotel

At Margaret & Edward streets; tel: 3221 1999; www.stamford.com.au; $$$$

An elegant and contemporary hotel with a lovely heritage facade, located on the banks of the Brisbane River. All 252 rooms in the modern high-rise building boast panoramic river views and are comfortable and spacious.

> Price for a double room for one night without breakfast:
>
> $$$$ over A$220
> $$$ A$150–220
> $$ A$80–150
> $ below A$80

Above from far left: Treasury Casino and Hotel; an opulent room within the hotel.

Other Options Comprehensive listings can be found in the RACQ (Royal Automobile Club of Queensland) *Accommodation Guide,* which covers the whole of Queensland. You can also get help at the regional and municipal information centres and their respective websites.

Treasury Casino and Hotel

130 William Street; tel: 3306 8888; www.conradtreasury.com.au; $$$$

An award-winning hotel located in the grand former Land Administration building, ideally situated in the heart of Brisbane with views of the river and South Bank across the street. Ornate and sumptuous heritage furnishings accentuate the hotel's opulent character, and the casino provides several dining and entertainment options.

Urban Hotel

345 Wickham Terrace; tel: 3831 6177; www.urbanbrisbane.com.au; $$–$$$

Centrally located and surrounded by parklands, the boutique Urban has comfortable if simple rooms with small private balconies. The in-house Gazebo restaurant and bar offers relaxed dining with a 'fusion' menu.

Moreton Island

Tangalooma Island Resort

tel: 3410 6000; www.tangalooma.com; $$$–$$$$

This efficient all-in-one, eco-friendly, family-focused resort offers numerous packages that include activities and tours such as the famous dolphin-feeding at dusk. Choose between hotel rooms, serviced apartments, villa units and fully self-contained houses with various levels of comforts and luxury. There are several beachside restaurants for casual dining.

Sunshine Coast

Breakfree French Quarter Resort

62 Hastings Street, Noosa Heads; tel: 5430 7100; www.frenchquarter.com.au; $$$

Right on Noosa's main drag and only 50m/yds from the beach, rooms here are either one- or two-bedroom apartments with kitchenette and balcony overlooking Hastings Street with all its fine eateries, or the landscaped gardens with a lagoon-style pool.

Halse Lodge

2 Halse Lane, Noosa Heads; tel: 5447 3377; www.halselodge.com.au; $

This backpackers' retreat and YHA hostel is in a rambling old Queenslander surrounded by rainforest gardens with the surf beach only 100m/yds away. As well as dorms there are twin and double rooms and a restaurant and bar. Very popular, so book ahead.

Noosa Village Motel

10 Hastings Street, Noosa Heads; tel: 5447 5800; www.noosavillage.com.au; $$

Price for a double room for one night without breakfast:	
$$$$	over A$220
$$$	A$150–220
$$	A$80–150
$	below A$80

Surprisingly affordable for its fantastic location, this modest motel offers a variety of spotless and comfortable rooms with kitchenettes and ceiling fans. With Hastings Street's restaurants, the beach and Noosa National Park just a short stroll away, this makes a great mid-range choice for families.

North Stradbroke Island

Stradbroke Island Beach Hotel and Spa Resort

East Coast Road, Point Lookout; tel: 3409 8188; www.stradbroke-hotel.com.au; $$$

Situated atop a headland and overlooking pristine beaches where you may glimpse a whale, the 'Straddie Pub' offers luxury ocean-facing apartments plus hotel rooms and suites. Minimum stays of two or three nights apply, and a potential drawback – or plus – is that the popular bar and restaurant keep the action busy and the noise levels high until midnight.

Gold Coast

Coolangatta YHA

230 Coolangatta Road, Bilinga; tel: 5536 7644; www.coolangattayha. com; $

Only 500m/yds from Coolangatta Airport and 150m/yds from the amazing surf of North Kirra Beach. Rooms range from dorms to singles, doubles and family rooms. Tour bookings, surfboard hire, surfing lessons and shuttles to the best breaks are all available. To say that this friendly hostel is surf-obsessed would be an understatement.

Courtyard Surfers Paradise Resort

At Surfers Paradise Boulevard and Hanlan Street, Surfers Paradise; tel: 5579 3499; www.marriott.com; $$$$

The 400-plus luxury rooms at this high-quality hotel are spread over 36 floors of a beachfront high-rise. Central to all the restaurants and attractions in Surfers Paradise, and with a lovely pool and spa, this a convenient and popular choice for families. For the best views of the ocean and surf, ask for a room from the 20th floor upwards.

Hill Haven Holiday Apartments

2 Goodwin Terrace, Burleigh Heads; tel: 5535 1055; www.hillhaven.com. au; $$$

Nestled into the headland and adjoining Burleigh Heads National Park, this block of spacious apartments is superbly positioned with restaurants and a renowned surf beach just a short stroll away. Beautifully furnished two- and three-bedroom apartments offer panoramic views over Surfers Paradise, the ocean and the hinterland from balconies. The three-night booking minimum in the low season rises to five nights in the holiday season.

Above from far left: Stamford Plaza superior room; the hotel's high-rise setting in Brisbane; apartment at the Tangalooma Island Resort on Moreton.

Oaks Calypso Plaza Resort

99 Griffith Street, Coolangatta; tel: 5599 0000; www.theoaksrhm.com. au; $$

An attractive, family-friendly, low-rise well away from the high-rise strip, very near the surf beach and airport. This well thought-out resort is equipped with a gym, games room and a lagoon-style swimming pool with waterslides. Rooms range from studios to one- and two-bedroom apartments. They regularly offer specials, so be sure to ask when you book.

Palazzo Versace

Sea World Drive, Main Beach; tel: 1800 098 000; www.palazzo versace.com; $$$$

The ultimate in 'Renaissance' splendour, luxury and immaculate service is expressed in this 205-room hotel, the first venture into hotels by Donatella Versace. Supposedly a six-star establishment, it has all the style and extravagance associated with the brand liberally embossed throughout.

Pelican Cove

At Back and Burrows streets, Surfers Paradise; tel: 1800 354 025; www.pelicancove.com.au; $$–$$$

This family-friendly resort has self-contained two- and three-bedroom units right on the Broadwater waterfront, with two saltwater swimming pools and spacious grounds. Just 10 minutes from Wet 'n' Wild, Dream-

world, Sea World and Movie World theme parks, and the tour desk sells discounted tickets.

Gold Coast Hinterland

Binna Burra Mountain Lodge

Lamington National Park; tel: 1300 246 622; www.binnaburralodge. com.au; $$$–$$$$

Perched on a hinterland ridge with sweeping views, this award-winning eco-lodge is a romantic retreat, offering log cabins with dinner, bed and breakfast, or just bed-and-breakfast packages. There are also campsites available, plus a restaurant, spa and nature trails.

Fraser Island

Kingfisher Bay Resort

North White Cliffs; tel: 4120 3333; www.kingfisherbay.com; $$$$

A well-appointed eco-resort that has hotel rooms, self-contained villas surrounded by rainforest, and multi-bedroom houses. The better rooms have sea views and spa baths. There are four swimming pools, four bars and four restaurants, and the resort has a helpful tour and activity desk.

Price for a double room for one night without breakfast:

$$$$	over A$220
$$$	A$150–220
$$	A$80–150
$	below A$80

Whitsunday Islands and Airlie Beach

Airlie Beach Hotel

At The Esplanade and Coconut Grove, Airlie Beach; tel: 4964 1999; www.airliebeachhotel.com.au; $$–$$$$

Absolutely prime seafront location with four-star facilities makes this one of the busier hotels in town, but justifiably so. Hotel rooms have either beach-view or town-view balconies and sleep either two or three people. Less expensive, three-star motel rooms do not have the balcony views. There are three restaurants on site, and the main drag is only a stroll away.

Coral Sea Resort

25 Oceanview Avenue, Airlie Beach; tel: 4964 1300; www.coralsearesort. com; $$$

The only absolute waterfront resort in Airlie Beach offers a range of apartment-style rooms, many with spa baths, near the Abel Point marina. The resort is just three minutes' stroll along a boardwalk from Airlie Beach's main drag. The setting is stunning, with a large pool, great patio café and bar, and the resort's own jetty doubles as a dining venue. The rooms range from one-bedroom hotel rooms to suites, apartments and penthouses.

Hamilton Island

Tel: 4946 9999; www.hamiltonisland. com.au; $$$$

There is a range of room types on this highly developed, self-contained island, all of which are expensive. Choose from the exclusive Qualia, Beach Club, Reef View Hotel, Whitsunday Holiday Apartments and the Palm Bungalows. The latter is the cheapest option, while Qualia occupies the other end of the spectrum. There's a staggering range of recreation and dining options, too.

Magnums Backpackers

366 Shute Harbour Road, Airlie Beach; tel: 4964 1199; www. magnums.com.au; $

The most central hostel at Airlie is also one of the friendliest. It offers dormitory, twin share and double accommodation, and the cheapest beer in town. There's a helpful tour desk, and it is right across the road from the swimming lagoon.

Cairns

Acacia Court Hotel

223–227 The Esplanade; tel: 4051 5011; www.acaciacourthotel.com: $$

The Acacia Court Hotel is just 2km (1¼ miles) from the city centre, a pleasant walk along The Esplanade. Rooms have queen-size beds, en suite bath or shower rooms, and balconies with either ocean or mountain views. There are also cheaper motel-style rooms. The on-site resataurant Charlie's has an all-you-can-eat buffet every night.

Above from far left: Palazzo Versace; oceanfront gazebo at the Coral Sea Resort.

Galvins Edge Hill B&B

61 Walsh Street; tel: 4032 1308; www.galvinsonedge.com.au; $$$

This welcoming B&B is in a genuine old Queenslander in a peaceful location. With a lounge and breakfast room that opens onto the natural-rock swimming pool, and just two bedrooms and a bathroom, only one family or group is booked at a time, so you have the whole place to yourselves.

Gilligan's Backpackers Hotel and Resort

57–89 Grafton Street; tel: 4041 6566; www.gilligansbackpackers.com.au; $–$$

This huge backpackers' resort offers economical dorm beds plus twin and double rooms, rowdy entertainment and a social soup of a swimming pool. All rooms are air-conditioned and have en suite bathrooms, and each floor has its own kitchen.

Shangri-La Hotel

The Marina, Pier Point Road; tel: 4031 1411; www.shangri-la.com/cairns; $$$–$$$$

Fronting the turquoise waters of Trinity Inlet and the Marlin Marina with its bobbing luxury flotilla, this luxury hotel has excellent views and a convenient location. Rooms and suites boast private balconies or patios and a range of leisure facilities, including a large swimming pool, in more than an acre of lush tropical gardens.

Port Douglas

Hibiscus Gardens Spa Resort

22 Owens Street; tel: 4099 5315; www.hibiscusportdouglas.com.au; $$$–$$$$

Set among exotic gardens with two pools, this neat hotel has a Balinese theme. Accommodation spans motel-style to three-bedroom apartments, some with private spas. And it is less than five minutes' walk to the beach and shops.

Daintree and Cape Tribulation

Cape Tribulation Beach House Resort

Cape Tribulation Road; tel: 4098 0030; www.capetribbeach.com.au; $–$$$

Situated 48km (30 miles) from the ferry terminal, this place provides dormitory and family cabins across eight price categories to cater for all budgets. Common areas include the saltwater swimming pool, the Sand Bar and Bistro, and communal kitchen and laundry facilities for self-caterers. It is located as close to the beach as the National Parks Authority will allow.

Daintree Eco Lodge & Spa

20 Daintree Road, Daintree; tel: 4098 6100; www.daintree-ecolodge.com.au; $$$$

Just 15 private cabins are offered at this luxurious nature retreat nestled into the rainforest a short drive from

Daintree village. It's not one for families, but a great romantic splurge with a well-being spa and restaurant that takes cues from the local environment and indigenous knowledge to create its Australian tropical cuisine.

Above from far left: Shangri-La Hotel, Cairns; pampering at the Daintree Eco Lodge.

Atherton Tablelands

Eden House Retreat and Mountain Spa

20 Gillies Highway, Yungaburra; tel: 4089 7000; www.edenhouse.com. au; $$–$$$

This exquisite heritage retreat offers secluded cottages and villas with private spas set in luxuriant gardens. Although aimed at couples looking for a relaxing escape, there is adequate accommodation for families as well. There's a restaurant and bar and the excellent Mountain Spa that offers a wide range of indulgent packages to pamper your body and soul.

Mission Beach

The Elandra at Mission Beach

Explorer Drive, South Mission Beach; tel: 4068 8154; www.elandraresorts. com; $$$–$$$$

The views from this resort-style hotel, on the southern headland above Mission Beach, are magnificent. The luxury accommodation with its chic African tribal theme is set amidst rainforest rich in wildlife, and the building is architecturally designed so that everybody enjoys privacy and an elevated ocean and beach view.

Scottys Mission Beach House

167 Reid Road; tel: 4068 8676; www.scottysbeachhouse.com.au; $

A very popular family-run backpackers' hostel opposite the beach, offering budget accommodation in either four-, six- or 12-person dormitories, female-only dorms and motel-style doubles. There's a swimming pool, free parking, guest kitchen, bar and bistro and lots of help with local activities.

Dunk Island

Dunk Island Resort

Tel: 4068 8199; www.dunk-island. com; $$$$

Just a 45-minute trip by ferry from Mission Beach is this family-friendly resort on a gorgeous tropical rainforest island. Rooms range from simple garden rooms to luxury beachfront suites, and there is a huge range of activities, including snorkelling trips, horse riding, nature walks, watersports, and even a children's club. You can choose packages that include meals and there are discounts for stays of four nights or more.

Price for a double room for one night without breakfast:	
$$$$	over A$220
$$$	A$150–220
$$	A$80–150
$	below A$80

In Brisbane and Cairns and along the coast where tourism is significant, you will have no trouble finding quality fresh food prepared with flair and usually with multicultural influences. In Brisbane, there are several restaurant neighbourhoods just a few minutes' cab drive or bus/ferry ride from the CBD *(see margin, opposite)*, while in Cairns, Shields Street is known as 'Eats Street', with more dining options along the boardwalk facing the Marlin Marina and along the Esplanade.

Brisbane

Aria Restaurant

Eagle Street Pier, Eagle Street; tel: 3233 2555; www.ariarestaurant. com; Mon–Fri noon–2.30pm, 5.30–10.30pm, Sat–Sun 5–10.30pm; $$$

With spectacular views over Story Bridge and the Brisbane River, Aria has an elegant contemporary menu devised by celebrity chef Matt Moran. Seafood and top-quality steaks dominate, but there are vegetarian options and delicate Asian interpretations. The innovative cuisine is matched to an extensive wine list, showcasing many of Australia's iconic wineries.

> Price range for a two-course meal for one including a glass of house wine:
>
> $$$ over A$60
> $$ A$40–60
> $ below $40

Augustine's on George

40 George Street; tel: 3221 9365; www.augustines.com.au; Mon–Fri noon–2.30pm & 6–10pm, Sat 6–10pm; $$$

Hong Kong expatriate Augustine Tso has been a flag on Brisbane's fine-dining map for more than 25 years. The quality at this snug restaurant has never wavered: thoughtful, flavoursome dishes that sit lightly on the palate. Entrées such as soufflé gruyère and truffle with baby salad and toasted hazelnuts set the scene for mains like barramundi fillet with citrus and herb crust, king prawns and beurre blanc.

Breakfast Creek Hotel

2 Kingsford Smith Drive, Albion; tel: 3262 95988; www.breakfast creekhotel.com; daily noon–2.30pm, 6–10.30pm; $$

The Brekkie's steaks are virtually the size of a dinner plate, and consistently thick, juicy and flavoursome. Choose your own from 12 premium cuts at the barbecue in the Beer Garden or visit the Spanish Garden Steakhouse for full table service and other menu items. But it's the steaks that make this place famous.

E'cco

At Boundary Street and Adelaide Street East; tel: 3831 8344; www. eccobistro.com; Tue–Fri noon–2.30pm & 6pm–late, Sat 6pm–late; $$$

One of Brisbane's most awarded bistros. Philip Johnson's mantra is simplicity, simplicity, simplicity. Settle in for field mushrooms, olive toast, rocket and parmesan, or try rare-seared wagyu beef salad with Asian herbs, chilli caramel and candied sesame seeds. And that's just for starters. Mains include grilled white fish, seafood paella, merguez sausage and saffron aioli.

Gambaro's Seafood Restaurant

33 Caxton Street, Petrie Terrace, Paddington; tel: 3369 9500; www.gambaros.com.au; Mon–Fri noon–2pm & 6pm–late, Sat 6pm–late; $$$

The Gambaro family have been in the seafood business since 1953, and Gambaro's has been a Brisbane institution since it opened in 1972. The seafood platters are a gastronomic delight, and from the tanks you can select Moreton Bay bugs, lobster and mud crabs. While seafood is what the restaurant specialises in, there are other options, including steak, chicken and pasta dishes.

Green Papaya

898 Stanley Street, East Brisbane; tel: 3217 3599; www.greenpapaya.com.au; Fri noon–2.30pm & 5.30–9.30pm, Tue–Thur & Sat–Sun 5.30–9.30pm; $$$

The Green Papaya offers a beguiling blend of classic and contemporary Vietnamese cuisine. Try the seafood stir-fry with lemon myrtle sauce, the Saigon rocket and crabmeat filling with prawn in crispy fried rice paper, or the bouillabaisse spiced with lemongrass, galangal and coriander. It is licensed and BYO, but the corkage is a whopping $6 per bottle.

Il Centro Restaurant

Eagle Street Pier, Eagle Street; tel: 3221 6090; www.il-centro.com.au; Sun–Fri noon–2.30pm & 5.30pm–late, Sat 5.30pm–late; $$$

Il Centro is one of a trio of quality restaurants overlooking the Brisbane River at the Eagle Street Pier complex. Alsace-born chef Romain Bapst is a master of texture and flavour, delivering an Italian-inspired menu with great skill. Expect wonderful seafood and pasta – try the celebrated lasagne *alla granseola* (sand crab lasagne) – plus prime cuts of steak.

Jade Buddha

Eagle Street Pier, Eagle Street; tel: 3221 2888; www.jadebuddha.com.au; daily 11.30am–late; $$$

With its pan-Asian cuisine using plenty of fresh seafood, plus colourful cocktails in the trendy Shadow Lounge, the 'Buddha' attracts Brisbane's glitterati. There are plenty of moreish bar snacks and light meals to kick the night off while feasting on excellent river and bridge views. Try the seafood laksa, chicken katsu curry or the Balinese-style lamb.

Above from far left: Aria; E'cco.

Where to Eat in Brisbane
Brisbane's foodie precincts include West End (diverse, with a pronounced Asian emphasis); Milton (deli-style cafés to silver-service dining, in a slightly more upmarket atmosphere); Brunswick Street, (cheap eats); and Chinatown Mall in Fortitude Valley (Brisbane's home of Asian cuisine). Downtown are South Bank and the Eagle Street Pier/ Riverside Centre, where several attractive and lively restaurants overlook the Brisbane River and Story Bridge.

Gold Coast

Absynthe

Q1 complex, 9 Hamilton Avenue, Surfers Paradise; tel: 5504 6466; www.absynthe.com.au; Fri noon–2pm & 6–9.30pm, Mon–Sat 6–9.30pm; $$$

Celebrated French chef Meyjitte Boughenout lends a dash of Gallic *élan* to the 80-storey Q1 building. His restaurant is famous for juxtaposing the most unlikely of flavours to create taste sensations that are as beguiling as they are unexpected. Ingredients include Périgord truffle, royal caviar and gold leaf accompanying fresh ingredients such as ocean trout, rabbit and duck sourced from all over Australia.

The Broadbeach Tavern

Oasis Shopping Centre, Old Burleigh Road, Broadbeach; tel: 5538 4111; www.broadbeachtavern.com.au; daily 11.30am–2.30pm, 5.30–8.30pm; $–$$

Choose simple, good-quality meals from a small and inexpensive menu including items such as burgers, fish and chips, and juicy steaks. The tavern is an unpretentious place where guest bands enliven the atmosphere most nights and stand-up merchants entertain on Wednesday comedy night.

Oskars on Burleigh

Burleigh Beach House, 43 Goodwin Terrace, Burleigh Heads; tel: 5576 3722; www.oskars.com.au; daily noon–2.30pm, 6–10pm; $$$

Oskars has been a Gold Coast institution for 28 years, and it is easy to see why. The seafood-dominated menu changes daily, but the twice-baked sand crab soufflé with tomato compote, rocket and walnut salad is a frequent entrée. The beach location, with sweeping ocean views north to Surfers Paradise, is a strong component of its appeal.

Ristorante Fellini

Marina Mirage, Seaworld Drive, Main Beach; tel: 5531 0300; www.fellini.com.au; daily noon–2.30pm, 6–10pm; $$–$$$

Brothers Carlo and Tony Percuoco dish up superb Italian cuisine within their elegant, award-winning restaurant. Try the pasta *linguette allo zafferano*: saffron-infused long flat pasta cooked with Moreton Bay bug meat in a light cream sauce. Like other creations on the menu, the dish makes a virtue of simplicity, and is a perennial favourite with regulars. The restaurant looks across the Southport Broadwater, and behind it stands the Percuoco's pasta shop, Pastificio Fellini, where the available lines include

Price range for a two-course meal for one including a glass of house wine:

$$$	over A$60
$$	A$40–60
$	below $40

ravioli filled with crabmeat and leek cooked in Sauvignon blanc.

Shuck

20 Tedder Avenue, Main Beach; tel: 5528 4286; www.shuck.com.au; daily noon–late; $$$

As the name implies, Shuck is noted for oysters, along with excellent seafood chowder, bouillabaisse, crab lasagne and... the ubiquitous steaks. Seating is mainly alfresco, with courtyard tables overlooking a passing parade of poseurs. The Mod Oz cuisine, open-air setting and general relaxed vibe make it exactly right for this trendy Gold Coast precinct.

Cairns

Café China

Rydges Plaza Complex, at Spence and Grafton Streets; tel: 4041 2828; www.cafechina.com.au; daily 11am–late; $$

Try delicious mainly Beijing and Hong Kong dishes, with some Szechuan menu entries, dim sum, seafood and noodles cooked in a healthy low-fat style with no added MSG. House specialties include salt-and-pepper mud crab, Peking duck and steamed coral trout. Owner Harry Sou makes sure that diners are well looked after.

Donnini's Ciao Italia

Shop 7K, The Pier Quayside; Wharf Street; tel: 4051 1133; daily 11am–late; $$

Consistently good and value-for-money Italian food, especially the pizza and pasta, with highlights listed on the daily specials board. A bonus is the boardwalk location, with a great view of activities at the marina while catching the sea breeze. The service is helpful and friendly.

Khin Kao Thai Restaurant

At Aplin and Grafton Streets; tel: 4031 8581; daily 11am–2pm, 5–10pm; $$

The best Thai restaurant in Cairns is a popular venue indeed with an extensive menu of all the favourites, such as Massaman, yellow, green and red curries, and featuring local seafood. Service is efficient and the prices are very reasonable, including a good-value daily lunch special.

Ochre Restaurant

43 Shields Street; tel: 4051 0100; www.ochrerestaurant.com.au; Mon–Fri noon–2.30pm & 6–10pm, Sat–Sun 6–10pm; $$$

In this multi-award-winning restaurant, creative modern Australian cuisine is offered with inventive flair that uses 40 different native ingredients to enhance dishes based on kangaroo, crocodile, beef, tropical fruit and local seafood. Try the kangaroo sirloin with *quandong* chilli glaze, and for dessert, wattleseed pavlova with Davidson plum sorbet, or check the daily specials board.

Above from far left: Oskars on Burleigh; Absynthe; Ochre Restaurant in Cairns.

In Brisbane the **Queensland Performing Arts Centre** (tel: 136 246; www.qpac.com.au) in South Bank is the major hub for the city's cultural entertainment; the following is but a very small selection of what else is on offer.

Don't look for wall-to-wall sophistication in northern Queensland; nightlife in Cairns, Airlie Beach and Mission Beach focuses on the backpacker party circuit, featuring themed nightclubs and barn-sized pubs with live entertainment.

In all Australian nightclubs, bars and casinos, entry is restricted to over-18s; the young and young-looking may have to show ID.

Brisbane

Brisbane Jazz Club

1 Annie Street, Kangaroo Point; tel: 3391 2006; www.brisbanejazzclub.com.au

Right beside the river near the Holman Street wharf, this characterful and intimate venue hosts occasional big-name acts, Brisbane's best traditional and contemporary jazz musicians and singers, and relaxed jam sessions. Check the website for the programme and session times.

Brisbane Powerhouse Centre for the Arts

119 Lamington Street, New Farm; tel: 3358 8622; www.brisbane powerhouse.com.au; box office Mon–Fri 9am–5pm, Sat noon–4pm

This world-class theatre, concert hall and experimental playhouse has an ever-changing repertoire and a focus on cutting-edge performances from Australia and overseas.

Cloudland

647 Ann Street, Fortitude Valley; tel: 3852 5000; www.cloudland.tv; Tue–Sun 11am–late

From outside, the spectacular geometric facade and rough wooden door give no indication that this is a nightspot, but inside a huge atrium shelters three levels of chic bars capped by a retractable roof. There are DJs and live entertainment along with reasonably priced drinks and a restaurant.

Family

8 McLachlan Street, Fortitude Valley; tel: 3852 5000; www.thefamily.com. au; Fri–Sun 9pm–5am

Family has been voted Australia's best nightclub, with six bars, four levels, three music genres, massive sound and light technology, two huge dance floors and the capacity for 2,000 patrons. It attracts international DJs, musicians and occasional eclectic acts.

Story Bridge Hotel

200 Main Street, Kangaroo Point; tel: 3391 2266; www.storybridge hotel.com.au; Mon–Thur 10am–midnight, Fri–Sat 10am–1.30am; Sun 8am–midnight

Situated under the famous bridge, this popular hotel has three bars and dining venues. Bands occasionally play Thursday to Saturday nights, and there's live jazz on Sunday afternoons.

The Zoo
711 Ann Street; tel: 3854 1381; www.thezoo.com.au; Wed–Sat
Brisbane's grand-daddy of live music venues champions indie bands, but also features DJs to broaden the musical mix (reggae, jazz, hip hop...).

Gold Coast

Dracula's Cabaret Restaurant
1 Hooker Boulevard, Broadbeach Waters; tel: 5575 1000; www.drac ulas.com.au; daily 6pm–midnight
Part of Australia's longest-established theatre-restaurant chain, Dracula's features a dinner-cabaret show with magic, puppetry, musical productions and great comedy, all with classic horror themes, including a ghost train. Not recommended for kids under 13 years.

The Gold Coast Arts Centre
135 Bundall Road, Surfers Paradise; tel: 5581 6500; www.gcac.com.au
The Coast's nocturnal culture revolves around this centre. Live performances are a blend of Australian and international, old and new: Thursday is 'unplugged' in the Basement, Friday is usually comedy night, and Saturday is jazz. There's also a café, films, theatre and a gallery.

Cairns

Reef Hotel Casino
35–41 Wharf Street; tel: 4030 8888; www.reefcasino.com.au
The casino has more than 500 gaming machines and more than 40 tables, as well as restaurants, bars and various kinds of live entertainment.

Port Douglas

Flames of the Forest
Tel: 4099 3144; www.flamesofthe forest.com.au; Thur–Sat
Dine in the rainforest and listen to Aboriginal stories: guests are picked up from their hotels from 6pm and transported to the Mowbray Valley, where flames light a path to a clearing and candles flicker beside a stream. More candles illuminate tables, immaculately set. It's *Lord of the Rings* meets *Alice in Wonderland*; an original and magical experience.

Karnak Playhouse
Upper Whyanbeel Road, Miallo; tel: 4098 8111; www.karnakplayhouse. com.au; evening performances May–Dec Wed and Sat.
Karnak is a little out of town, but well worth the trip, and there are bus connections from Port Douglas for performances. A range of plays is presented in a magnificent rainforest amphitheatre, which seats 500. It's also open daily during the day for light lunches, made from organic produce grown on-site, and for afternoon tea.

Above from far left: Brisbane Powerhouse; Flames of the Forest.

What's On?
Nightlife venues and session times are listed in the daily *Courier-Mail*, and there are free publications such as *Rave*, *Time Off* and *Scene*, which can be picked up at venues and cafés. Try also www. brisbane247.com. Listings for the Cairns area can be found in Friday's *Cairns Post*.

CREDITS

Insight Step by Step Brisbane, Cairns and the Great Barrier Reef
Written by: Lindsay Brown
Additional text by: Cathy Finch
Senior Commissioning Editor: Alexander Knights
Series Editor: Clare Peel
Cartography Editors: Zoë Goodwin and James Macdonald
Map Production: Phoenix Mapping
Picture Manager: Steven Lawrence
Art Editor: Ian Spick
Deputy Art Editor: Richard Cooke
Photography: All photography by Peter Stuckings/APA except: Alamy 17, 53; ARIA Restaurant 6-4, 118; AWL Images 70, 84; Brisbane Powerhouse 122; Cairns Tropical Zoo 82-1; Cairns Wildlife Dome 74-1,3; CITY publicity 16-3, 120-2; Coffee Works Experience 89, 92-2; Coral Princess Cruises 4-4, 7-5, 26-1, 28-2, 32-2; Coral Sea Resort 116; Jerry Dennis/APA 16-2; Mary Evans Picture Library 30; George Favios 119; Flames of the Forest 123; Fotolia 95; Glyn Genin/APA 8-7, 19-2; iStockphoto.com 6-1, 7-4, 15-1, 49-2, 64-1, 94, 98-3, 100; Christopher Frederick Jones/QPAC 42-2; Jungle Surfing 87-1,2; Kingfisher Bay Resort 63, 64-2; Kuranda, Village in the Rainforest 78-1; Kuranda Scenic Railway 79; Kuranda Skyrail 76; Nerada Tea 92-3; Ochre Restaurant 15-1, 121; Oskars Restaurant 32-7, 120-1; Palazzo Versace 114; PCL 85; QPAC 21; Queensland Folk Federation Inc 20; Quicksilver and Great Adventures 28-1,3, 29; Raging Thunder 23; Rainforest Habitat Wildlife Sanctuary 80; Shangri-La Hotels & Resorts 116; Spirit of Freedom 26-2, 27; Stamford Hotels and Resorts 112-1,2; State Library of Queensland 31; Tangalooma Island Resort 6-2, 13, 44/45, 45-1, 46-1, 113; Tanks Arts Centre 7-3; Tjapukai Aboriginal Cultural Park, Cairns 8-4; Tourism Port Douglas & Daintree 22-2, 81, 98-4; Tourism Queesland 2-6, 8-1,5, 14, 28-4, 32-4, 45-2, 46-2, 47, 52, 54/55(all), 65, 66, 67, 68/69, 83, 96/97(all), 117; Treasury Casino and Hotel 111; Warner Village Theme Parks 2-2, 6-3, 8-6, 24, 25-1,2, 98-6
Front cover: main image: photolibrary; bottom left and right: iStockphoto.com.
Printed by: CTPS-China

© 2010 APA Publications GmbH & Co. Verlag KG (Singapore branch)

First Edition 2010

CONTACTING THE EDITORS

We would appreciate it if readers would alert us to errors or outdated information by writing to us at insight@apaguide.co.uk or APA Publications, PO Box 7910, London SE1 1WE, UK.

www.insightguides.com

DISTRIBUTION

Worldwide

APA Publications GmbH & Co. Verlag KG (Singapore branch)
7030 Ang Mo Kio Ave 5
08-65 Northstar @ AMK
Singapore 569880
Tel: (65) 6570 1051
E-mail: apasin@singnet.com.sg

UK and Ireland

GeoCenter International Ltd
Meridian House, Churchill Way West
Basingstoke, Hampshire, RG21 6YR
Tel: (44) 01256 817 987
E-mail: sales@geocenter.co.uk

United States

Langenscheidt Publishers, Inc.
36–36 33rd Street, 4th Floor
Long Island City, NY 11106
Tel: (1) 718 784 0055
E-mail: orders@langenscheidt.com

Australia

Universal Publishers
1 Waterloo Road, Macquarie Park, NSW 2113
Tel: (61) 2 9857 3700
E-mail: sales@universalpublishers.com.au

New Zealand

Hema Maps New Zealand Ltd (HNZ)
Unit 2, 10 Cryers Road
East Tamaki, Auckland 2013
Tel: (64) 9 273 6459
E-mail: sales.hema@clear.net.nz

INDEX